KIDS LOVE KENTUCKY

A PARENT'S GUIDE TO EXPLORING FUN PLACES IN KENTUCKY WITH CHILDREN. . .YEAR ROUND!

Kids Love Publication
1985 Dina Court
Columbus, OH 43235

www.kidslovepublications.com

W9-BSW-907

Dedicated to the Families
of Kentucky

© Copyright 2004, Kids Love Publications

For the latest major updates corresponding to the pages in this book visit our website:
www.kidslovepublications.com

- ❑ *REMEMBER: Museum exhibits change frequently. Check the site's website before you visit to note any changes. Also, HOURS and ADMISSIONS are subject to change at the owner's discretion. If you are tight on time or money, check the attraction's website or call before you visit.*
- ❑ *INTERNET PRECAUTION: All websites mentioned in KIDS LOVE KENTUCKY have been checked for appropriate content. However, due to the fast-changing nature of the Internet, we strongly urge parents to preview any recommended sites and to always supervise their children when on-line.*

ISBN# 0-9726854-3-X
KIDS ♥ KENTUCKY ™ Kids Love Publications

TABLE OF CONTENTS

State Map

(With Major Routes and Cities Marked)

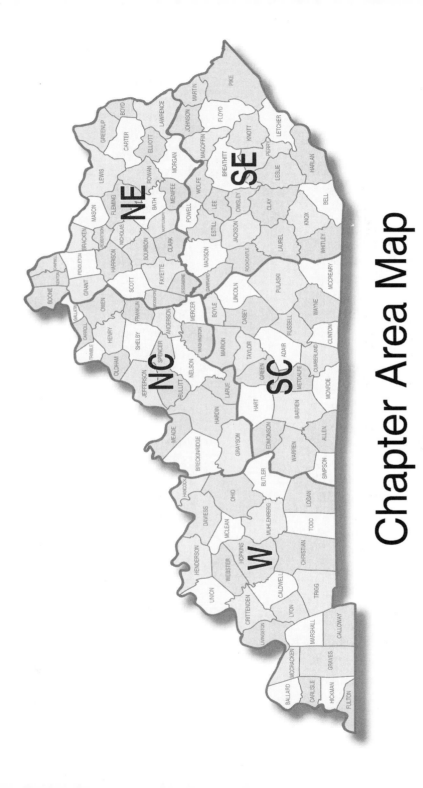

Chapter Area Map

CITY INDEX (Listed by City & Area)

CITY INDEX (Listed by City & Area)

Acknowledgements

We are most thankful to be blessed with our parents, Barbara (Darrall) Callahan & George and Catherine Zavatsky who help us every way they can – researching, proofing and babysitting. More importantly, they are great sounding boards and offer unconditional support. So many places around Kentucky remind us of family vacations years ago...

We also want to express our thanks to the many Convention & Visitor Bureaus' staff for providing the attention to detail that helps to complete a project. We felt very welcome during our travels in Kentucky and would be proud to call it home!

Our own kids, Jenny and Daniel, were delightful and fun children during our trips across the state. What a joy it is to be their parents...we couldn't do it without them as our "kid-testers"!

We both sincerely thank each other – our partnership has created an even greater business/personal "marriage" with lots of exciting moments, laughs, and new adventures in life woven throughout. Above all, we praise the Lord for His so many blessings through the last few years. God does answer prayer...all prayer, *eventually*!

We think Kentucky is a wonderful, friendly area of the country with more activities than you could imagine. Our sincere wish is that this book will help everyone "fall in love" with Kentucky.

In a Hundred Years...

It will not matter, The size of my bank account...
The kind of house that I lived in, the kind of car that I drove...
But what will matter is...
That the world may be different
Because I was important in the life of a child.

- *author unknown*

HOW TO USE THIS BOOK

If you are excited about discovering Kentucky, this is the book for you and your family! We've spent over a thousand hours doing all the scouting, collecting and compiling *(and most often visiting!)* so that you could spend less time searching and more time having fun.

Here are a few hints to make your adventures run smoothly:

- ❏ Consider the **child's age** before deciding to take a visit.
- ❏ Know **directions** and parking. Call ahead (or visit the company's website) if you have questions *and* bring this book. Also, don't forget your camera! *(please honor rules regarding use)*.
- ❏ **Estimate the duration** of the trip. Bring small surprises (favorite juice boxes) travel books, and toys.
- ❏ Call ahead for **reservations** or details, if necessary.
- ❏ Most listings are **closed major holidays** unless noted.
- ❏ Make a **family "treasure chest"**. Decorate a big box or use an old popcorn tin. Store memorabilia from a fun outing, journals, pictures, brochures and souvenirs. Once a year, look through the "treasure chest" and reminisce. "Kids Love Travel Memories!" is an excellent travel journal & scrapbook that your family can create. *(See the order form in back of this book)*.
- ❏ Plan **picnics** along the way. Many Historical Society sites and state parks are scattered throughout Kentucky. Allow time for a rural/scenic route to take advantage of these free picnic facilities.
- ❏ Some activities, especially tours, require **groups** of 10 or more. To participate, you may either ask to be part of another tour group or get a group together yourself (neighbors, friends, organizations). If you arrange a group outing, most places offer discounts.
- ❏ For the latest **updates** corresponding to the pages in this book, visit our website: **www.kidslovepublications.com.**
- ❏ Each chapter represents an area of the state. Each listing is further identified by city, zip code, and place/event name. Our popular **Activity Index** in the back of the book **lists places by Activity Heading** (i.e. State History, Tours, Outdoors, Museums, etc.).

MISSION STATEMENT

At first glance, you may think that this is a book that just lists hundreds of places to travel. While it is true that we've invested thousands of hours of exhaustive research (*and drove over 3000 miles in Kentucky*) to prepare this travel resource...just listing places to travel is <u>not</u> the mission statement of these projects.

As children, Michele and I were able to travel extensively throughout the United States. We consider these family times some of the greatest memories we cherish today. We, quite frankly, felt that most children had this opportunity to travel with their family as we did. However, as we became adults and started our own family, we found that this wasn't necessarily the case. We continually heard friends express several concerns when deciding how to spend "quality" and "quantity" family time. 1) What to do? 2) Where to do it? 3) How much will it cost? 4) How do I know that my kids will enjoy it?

Interestingly enough, as we compare our experiences with our families when we were kids, many of our fondest memories were not made at an expensive attraction, but rather when it was least expected.

It is our belief and mission statement that if you as a family will study and <u>use</u> the contained information <u>to create family memories,</u> these memories will grow a stronger, tighter family. Our ultimate mission statement is, that your children will develop a love and a passion for quality family experiences that they can pass to another generation of family travelers.

We thank you for purchasing this book, and we hope to see you on the road (*and hearing your travel stories!*) God bless your journeys and happy exploring!

- George, Michele, Jenny and Daniel

GENERAL INFORMATION

Call *(or visit the websites)* for the services of interest. Request to be added to their mailing lists.

- ❑ Canoe Kentucky (800) K-CANOE -1 or **www.canoeky.com**
- ❑ Kentucky Arts Council, **www.kyarts.org**
- ❑ Kentucky Bicycle Tours (800) 225-8747
- ❑ Kentucky Division of Water (502) 564-3410
- ❑ Kentucky Roadside Farm Markets **www.kyfb.com/roadside.htm**
- ❑ Kentucky State Parks (800) 255-Park or **www.state.ky.us/agencies/parks/parkhome.htm**
- ❑ Kentucky Tourism Council, **www.kentuckytourism.com** or (800) 225-8747
- ❑ Kentucky Trails Guide (800) 225-8747
- ❑ **NC** - Lake Cumberland & Big South Fork Area (800) 642-6287
- ❑ **NC** - Louisville MetroParks & Recreation (502) 456-8100
- ❑ **NC** - Oldham County Parks (502) 222-5933
- ❑ **NE** - Fayette County Parks & Recreation (859) 288-2900 or **www.lfucg.com/parksrec/**
- ❑ **NE** - Lexington CVB (800) 845-3959 or **www.visitlex.com**

STATE NATURE PRESERVES

- ❑ Phone: (502) 573-2886 **Web: wwwkynaturepreserves.org**
- ❑ Hours: Dawn to dusk, daily.
- ❑ Admission: FREE
- ❑ Miscellaneous: Open to the public for hiking, birding and nature study.

NC - <u>VERNON-DOUGLAS STATE NATURE PRESERVE</u> - Elizabethtown, off KY 583. Mature second growth forest with rich array of spring wildflowers.

State Nature Preserves *(cont.)*

NC - <u>BEARGRASS CREEK STATE NATURE PRESERVE</u> at the Louisville Nature Center - Louisville, 1297 Trevilian Way. (502) 458-1328. Over 40 acres of mature forest, adjacent to Creason Park, popular for birding in an urban setting.

NE - <u>BOONE COUNTY CLIFFS STATE NATURE PRESERVE</u> - Burlington, I-75 to KY 18 west. 20-40' cliffs formed from the gravel washed out of melting glaciers north of the area can be seen.

NE - <u>DINSMORE WOODS STATE NATURE PRESERVE</u> - Burlington, I-75 exit 181 to KY 18 west. Park at Middle Creek Park. Fairly undisturbed old growth mixed hardwood forest which hosts various spring wildflowers.

NE - <u>QUIET TRAILS STATE NATURE PRESERVE</u> - Cynthiana, off Pugh's Ferry Road, near Sunrise, on the Licking river. Birds, trees & wildflowers, over 20 species of mussels come from the river.

NE - <u>JESSE STUART STATE NATURE PRESERVE</u> - Greenup, West Hollow Road, off KY 1. Known as W-Hollow, it was home to the internationally known author, Jesse Stuart.

NE - <u>JIM BEAM NATURE PRESERVE</u> - Nicholasville, US 27 to Hall Lane (near Camp Nelson) to Payne Lane. Protecting a portion of the Palisades of the Kentucky River, this is a feeding habitat for rare bat species.

NE - <u>SALLY BROWN NATURE PRESERVE</u> - Nicholasville, US 27 to KY 1845 west to Camp Dick Fire Station left to High Bridge Road right to Bowman's Road right. Protects forests and 400 plant species in the Kentucky River Palisades.

NE - <u>TOM DORMAN STATE NATURE PRESERVE</u> - Nicholasville, US 27S to KY 1845. Forested slopes of spring wildflowers on spectacular 300' cliffs across the Kentucky River.

SE - <u>PILOT KNOB STATE NATURE PRESERVE</u> - Clay City, Mountain Pkwy, exit 16. One of the tallest knobs in the Cumberland Plateau. It's considered to be the place where Daniel Boone first stood and looked over the Bluegrass. Hiking here, too.

SE - <u>BAD BRANCH STATE NATURE PRESERVE</u> - Whitesburg, KY 932. Over 1000 acres of forested gorge containing a 60 foot waterfall, rare plants and animals.

W - <u>METROPOLIS LAKE STATE NATURE PRESERVE</u> - Paducah, off KY 996. Find five species of rare fish, beaver wintering place for bald eagles in a lake ringed with balk cypress and swamp tupelo.

W - <u>LOGAN COUNTY - GLADE STATE NATURE PRESERVE</u> - Russellville, off US 68/KY 80. Over 40 acres with limestone glades and a 810 foot knob. The rocky slopes are adorned with prairie grasses and rare plants like Carolina Larkspur, Glade violet and Fame flower.

FERRY SERVICES

NE - <u>ANDERSON FERRY</u> - Florence, KY8. Crosses Ohio River to US 50 in Ohio. Hours 6:00am-8:00pm (November-April) and 6:00am-9:30pm (May-October). Open 7:00am on Sundays & holidays. Fare: $3.00 per car.

NE - <u>VALLEY VIEW FERRY</u> - Nicholasville, KY 169E at the Kentucky River. The oldest continuous business in Kentucky since 1785. FREE.

SC - <u>CUMBERLAND RIVER FERRY</u> - Tompkinsville, KY 214. Kentucky's only state-operated ferry running 24 hours a day to scenic Turkey Neck Bend.

W - <u>HICKMAN-DORENA FERRY</u> - Hickman, Off KY 94. Ferry crosses the Mississippi river from Hickman to Dorena, MO. Runs daily except Christmas. 7:00am-6:15pm (April-October), 7:00am-5:00pm (November-March). Fare $8.00 per car.

W - <u>CAVE IN ROCK FERRY</u> - Marion, KY 91. Crosses the Ohio River to Illinois. FREE

KENTUCKY DEPARTMENT OF FISH & WILDLIFE RESOURCES

❑   Phone: (502) 564-4336 or (800) 858-1549
   Web: www.kdfwr.state.ky.us

NC - <u>FRANKFORT FISH HATCHERY</u> - Frankfort, Indian Gap Road, north off US 127 near Swallowfield. 45 rearing ponds, hatching house, and feed office occupy the land where fish are raised to stock farm ponds and public lakes and for research.

NE - <u>CAMP ROBERT WEBB CONSERVATION EDUCATION CENTER</u> - Grayson. 460 acres of deer and turkey. Vehicle traffic only. Year round Monday-Friday 8:00am-4:00pm.

W - <u>CAMP JOHN CURRIE CONSERVATION EDUCATION CENTER</u> - Benton, US 68 east on KY 962. Children's conservation camp June-August.

W - <u>SLOUGHS PUBLIC WILDLIFE AREA</u> - Henderson, Sauerheber Unit, on KY 268 northwest of Geneva. Almost 2000 acres where up to 30,000 Canadian geese and 10,000 ducks winter annually, with an observation platform. Kentucky's largest great blue heron rookery. Open mid-March to mid-October.

Check out these businesses / services in your area for tour ideas:

AIRPORTS

All children love to visit the airport! Why not take a tour and understand all the jobs it takes to run an airport? Tour the terminal, baggage claim, gates and security / currency exchange. Maybe you'll even get to board a plane.

ANIMAL SHELTERS

Great for the would-be pet owner. Not only will you see many cats and dogs available for adoption, but a guide will show you the clinic and explain the needs of a pet. Be prepared to have the children "fall in love" with one of the animals while they are there!

BANKS

Take a "behind the scenes" look at automated teller machines, bank vaults and drive-thru window chutes. You may want to take this tour and then open a savings account for your child.

CITY HALLS

Halls of Fame, City Council Chambers & Meeting Room, Mayor's Office and famous statues.

ELECTRIC COMPANY / POWER PLANTS

Modern science has created many ways to generate electricity today, but what really goes on with the "flip of a switch". Because coal can be dirty, wear old, comfortable clothes. Coal furnaces heat water, which produces steam, that propels turbines, that drives generators, that make electricity.

FIRE STATIONS

Many Open Houses in October, Fire Prevention Month. Take a look into the life of the firefighters servicing your area and try on their gear. See where they hang out, sleep and eat. Hop aboard a real-life fire engine truck and learn fire safety too.

HOSPITALS

Some Children's Hospitals offer pre-surgery and general tours.

NEWSPAPERS

You'll be amazed at all the new technology. See monster printers and robotics. See samples in the layout department and maybe try to put together your own page. After seeing a newspaper made, most companies give you a free copy (dated that day) as your souvenir. National Newspaper Week is in October.

RESTAURANTS

PIZZA HUT & PAPA JOHN'S

❑   Participating locations

Telephone the store manager. Best days are Monday, Tuesday and Wednesday mid-afternoon. Minimum of 10 people. Small charge per person. All children love pizza – especially when they can create their own! As the children tour the kitchen, they learn how to make a pizza, bake it, and then eat it. The admission charge generally includes lots of creatively made pizzas, beverage and coloring book.

KRISPY KREME DONUTS

❑   Participating locations

Get an "inside look" and learn the techniques that make these donuts some of our favorites! Watch the dough being made in "giant" mixers, being formed into donuts and taking a "trip" through the fryer. Seeing them being iced and topped with colorful sprinkles is always a favorite of the kids. Contact your local store manager. They prefer Monday or Tuesday. Free.

SUPERMARKETS

Kids are fascinated to go behind the scenes of the same store where Mom and Dad shop. Usually you will see them grind meat, walk into large freezer rooms, watch cakes and bread bake and receive free samples along the way. Maybe you'll even get to pet a live lobster!

TV / RADIO STATIONS

Studios, newsrooms, Fox kids clubs. Why do weathermen never wear blue clothes on TV? What makes a "DJ's" voice sound so deep and smooth?

WATER TREATMENT PLANTS

A giant science experiment! You can watch seven stages of water treatment. The favorite is usually the wall of bright buttons flashing as workers monitor the different processes.

U.S. MAIN POST OFFICES

Did you know Ben Franklin was the first Postmaster General (over 200 years ago)? Most interesting is the high-speed automated mail processing equipment. Learn how to address envelopes so they will be sent quicker (there are secrets). To make your tour more interesting, have your children write a letter to themselves and address it with colorful markers. Mail it earlier that day and they will stay interested trying to locate their letter in all the high-speed machinery.

Chapter 1
Area - North Central (NC)

Our Favorites...

* My Old Kentucky Home - Bardstown
* Kentucky History Center - Frankfort
* Rebecca Ruth Candy - Frankfort
* Salato Wildlife Education Center - Frankfort
* "Daniel Boone - The Man & The Legend" and
  Old Fort Harrod - Harrodsburg
* Lincoln Birthplace & Museum - Hodgenville
* American Printing House for the Blind - Louisville
* Louisville Slugger Museum - Louisville
* Pottery Tours - Louisville
* Kentucky Railway Museum - New Haven

*Pioneer Cookin'
with Daniel & Jenny
- Old Fort Harrod*

BARDSTOWN TOURMOBILE

107 East Stephen Foster Avenue (Tourist & Convention Commission)

Bardstown 40004

❑   Phone: (502) 348-4877 or (800) 638-4877
     Web: www.bardstowntourism.com
❑   Admission: $1.00 per person
❑   Tours: Monday-Saturday at 9:30am and 1:00pm.(June-August)

The tourmobile leaves from the commission for a 45 minute trip offering an introduction to the town. Families can opt to not stop at the Distillery on weekdays. This is a good way to get oriented to the area before you explore on your own and the staff are very welcoming.

CIVIL WAR MUSEUM

310 East Broadway (Rte. 60 exit 25 or I-65S exit 112)

Bardstown 40004

❑   Phone: (502) 349-0291. **Web: www.bardstown.com/~civilwar/**
❑   Hours: Monday-Saturday 10:00am-5:00pm, Sunday Noon-
     5:00pm (March-December). Rest of Year, weekends only.
     Closed New Years, Thanksgiving, and Christmas
❑   Admission: $5.00 adult, $4.00 senior (62+), $2.50 child (7-15).
❑   Miscellaneous: The Women in Civil War Museum is just up the
     street and operated by the same folks. Learn why early nurses
     were only nuns or plain spinsters; learn why women were the
     ones to realize more sanitary conditions were needed (famous
     Clara Barton, Elizabeth Blackwell); and especially learn why
     women were the best spies! Old Bardstown recreated Village is
     next door with authentic cabins to peek in. Separate small
     admission for self-guided tours of either of these other facilities.

See artifacts and photographs from Civil War battles fought in Georgia, Kentucky, Tennessee, Mississippi and Missouri. Also see rare flags, uniforms, maps, both North and South weapons and medical equipment. Trace the progression of the war, chronologically (easy to follow). They also have a campsite featuring a wagon actually used during a conflict on a battlefield. Here's some questions to answer when you tour: Why did West Virginia form as a separate state because of the Civil War? The book "Uncle Tom's Cabin" came out before the war started - did the author start the war? If you were a captain, how many buttons would you wear? Red, Yellow or Blue trim on a uniform - what does it mean? Injured in the war? (be careful, they loved to amputate)! Would you want to be a drummer boy? Before you leave, be sure to ask the story about the US belt buckle turned upside down. This museum was voted the 4th best Civil War museum in the nation.

MY OLD KENTUCKY HOME STATE PARK

US 150 Springfield Road (off the Bluegrass Pkwy, just east of downtown)

Bardstown 40004

❑   Phone: (502) 348-3502 or (800) 323-7803
   Web: www.state.ky.us/agencies/parks/kyhome.htm
❑   Hours: Daily 8:30am-6:15pm (June-August). Daily 9:00am-
   4:45pm (September-May). Closed Thanksgiving, week of
   Christmas and New Years.
❑   Admission: $4.50 adult, $4.00 senior (62+), $2.50 child (6-12).
❑   Miscellaneous: Gift shop, picnic, playground and camping. Tours
   every fifteen minutes.

The stately Georgian Colonial mansion is most famous because it is the inspiration for Stephen Foster's famous ballad "My Old Kentucky Home" - the official Kentucky state song. It was the home of Judge John Rowan whose Pittsburgh cousin, Stephen Foster, visited in 1852. Visit the days of the antebellum South as costumed guides escort you through the restored mansion, formal gardens, carriage house and smokehouse. Here are some unique things for the kids to look for while on tour: 13 foot high and 13 inch thick walls, 13 windows and 13 steps because of the 13 original colonies; see the "napping couch and Day Bed"; look for the "hip bath" for bathing in the kids' rooms; learn why children ate upstairs in the hallway; or look for the picture that follows you.

OLD TALBOTT TAVERN

107 West Stephen Foster Avenue (Court Square)

Bardstown 40004

❑   Phone: (800) 4-Tavern **Web: www.talbotts.com**

❑   Hours: Lunch and Dinner daily.

❑   Admission: Moderate to high priced menu.

❑   Miscellaneous: Bed & Breakfast and Gift Shop. Just browse if you like. Another place you can get a Kentucky Hot Brown.

Mid-America's oldest stagecoach stop where historic recipe meals are still served today. It's the oldest inn (1779) in continuous operation located west of the Alleghenies. Notables such as Louis Phillippe, John Audubon, and George Rogers Clark rested here on their journeys and you can see bullet holes shot by Jesse James! Choose from Fried Green Tomatoes, Burgoo, Mrs. Eleanor's Fried Chicken or Country Ham. After you order (or while you're waiting to be seated), take a self-guided look around. Although it's historic, it's unusually very kid-friendly. Wait staff are dressed in period and there's a great, fun children's menu.

STEPHEN FOSTER - THE MUSICAL

US 150 east of downtown (Bluegrass Pkwy. On grounds of "My Old Kentucky Home")

Bardstown 40004

❑   Phone: (502) 348-5971 or (800) 626-1563
Web: www.stephenfoster.com

❑   Hours: Tuesday-Sunday 8:30pm nightly (outdoor theatre, indoors if inclement weather). Saturday matinees at 2:00pm, indoors. (early June-late August). Wednesday, Thursday and Sunday evening shows are usually another famous musical vs. Stephen Foster. Check website for details of specific dates. EDT

❑   Admission: $15.00-$20.00 adult, ~ Half price for child (7-12). FREE for children 6 and under.

Stephen Foster - The Musical (cont.)

❑   Miscellaneous: The shows last over 2 hours. You may want to consider your child's attention span - especially late evening.

Performed under the stars for a romantic setting, this is a good follow up to your tour of My Old Kentucky Home up on the hill above the theatre. Spectacular period costumes, lively music, dances and more than 50 toe-stomping Foster songs including "Camptown Races" and "Oh, Susanna" - everyone knows them. Did you know Foster was America's first great composer?

TRIMBLE COUNTY OLD STONE JAIL & COUNTY COURTHOUSE

Court Street

Bedford 40006

❑   Phone: (800) 325-4290
❑   Hours: Monday-Friday 9:00am-5:00pm, Sat/Sun Noon -5:00pm.
❑   Admission: FREE

The 1880 courthouse and jail on the courthouse lawn is where the abolitionist Delia Webster, of the Underground Railroad, was imprisoned prior to being sent north by horseback. There's a museum and visitor's center also.

GENERAL BUTLER STATE RESORT PARK

PO Box 325 (I-71 at Carrollton - KY 227, 44 miles northeast of Louisville)

Carrollton 41008

❑   Phone: (502) 732-4384 or (866) GO-Butler (reservations)
    Web: www.kystateparks.com/genbutlr.htm
❑   Miscellaneous: Play it Again in the Park evening concerts (1st & 3rd Saturdays June-October).

This resort pays tribute to one of Kentucky's foremost military families, namely General William Orlando Butler. Beginning in colonial times through the Civil War, the military fame of the Butler family is known well and displayed at the Butler-Turpin Historic House. See the 1859 furnished home full of heirlooms

(Tours are February-December, three times daily for $1-3 admission). Also in the park is a hilltop lodge (53 rooms), short nature trails, tennis, cottages, a campground, a marina, rental boats, a pool and beach, mini-golf and recreation programs.

BERNHEIM FOREST

KY 245 (I-65 exit 112)

Clermont 40110

☐ Phone: (502) 955-8512 **Web: www.bernheim.org**

☐ Hours: Center, Daily 9:00am-5:00pm. Park, 7:00am to sunset. Closed Christmas and New Year's.

☐ Admission: Only charged Saturday, Sunday & Holidays. $5.00 per vehicle.

The official state arboretum with 2000 plants identified, a 14,000 acre forest, 3.5 miles of hiking trails, a fishing lake and visitors center. Take the auto tour of sculpture (we liked "Emerging", with its "pockets" of peeping holes) or stop in the Birds of Prey Building or Live Deer Pen. Get a Scavenger Hunt list before you hit the trails.

FREEMAN LAKE PARK

North US 31 W

Elizabethtown 42701

☐ Phone: (270) 765-2173 or (800) 437-0092

☐ Hours: Park open 8:00am-dusk. Homes open Saturday 10:00am-6:00pm, Sunday 1:00-6:00pm (June-September).

☐ Admission: Donations

On the campus of this park are three historic homes. The Lincoln Heritage House is a double log house crafted in part by Abraham Lincoln's father. The Sarah Bush Johnston Lincoln Memorial Cabin is a replica of the home of Sarah Bush Johnston's Elizabethtown home at the time she married Thomas Lincoln. Finally, the One Room School House was originally built in Summitt, KY in 1892 and considered the finest school in the county. The park also has fishing, playgrounds, picnic areas, canoe, rowboat, and pedal boat rental.

HISTORIC DOWNTOWN ELIZABETHTOWN WALKING TOUR

Downtown, **Elizabethtown** 42701

- ❑ Phone: (270) 765-2175 or (800) 437-0092
- ❑ Hours: Thursday at 7:00pm (June-August)
- ❑ Admission: FREE

The tour walks along 25 historic sites and buildings. Along the way, historical characters dramatically reveal their part in the town's history (with characters like General Custer). It's a whimsical "meet and greet" and a great way for kids to understand the personalities behind the history.

SWOPE'S CARS OF YESTERYEAR MUSEUM

1100 North Dixie Avenue (US 31W)

Elizabethtown 42701

- ❑ Phone: (270) 765-2181. **Web: www.swopemuseum.com**
- ❑ Hours: Monday-Saturday 9:00am-5:00pm. Closed Sundays and holidays.
- ❑ Admission: FREE

Wonderful machines of yesteryear (approx. 50) are on display. Most of the cars are from the 20s, 30s and 40s, and even a few from the 50s and 60s. Good nostalgia walk with grandparents at the lead. Take the time to listen to their memories…

ROUGH RIVER DAM STATE RESORT PARK

450 Lodge Road (Western Parkway to KY 79 north at Caneyville)

Falls of Rough 40119

- ❑ Phone: (270) 257-2311 or (800) 325-1713
  www.kystateparks.com/agencies/parks/roughrv2.htm
  www.pineknob.com
- ❑ Miscellaneous: Pine Knob Theatre - musical comedy and folklore, Friday & Saturday nights, June-September. Phone: (270) 879-8190. All seats $10.00. Reservations are not required unless groups.

For updates visit our website: www.kidslovepublications.com

Fine fishing waters can be found in the deep waters of Rough River. Fishing or not, there's also boat rentals, a lodge, cottages, dining, a beach, campgrounds, some hiking trails, tennis, golf, mini-golf and recreation programs surrounding the approximately 5000 acre lake. Enjoy the history of the area at old Falls of Rough, a quaint 19th century mill community.

GOLD VAULT - US BULLION DEPOSITORY

(View the Vault from US 31W and Bullion Blvd. On Fort Knox)

Fort Knox 40121

❑   Phone: (800) 334-7540

Constructed in 1936 at a cost of $560,000, the 2 level vault with door (weighing 20 tons) is guarded 24 hours a day. Made of granite, steel and concrete, its dimensions are 105 by 121 feet. Gold in the depository is in the form of standard mint bars somewhat smaller than a building brick - each brick weighs about 27.5 pounds. The Mint is guarded 24 hours a day. No visitors are allowed (unless you are a United States President or high level cabinet member)...but pictures may be taken of the outside of the building.

PATTON MUSEUM OF CAVALRY & ARMOR

4554 Fayette Avenue

Fort Knox 40121

❑   Phone: (502) 624-3812. **Web: www.generalpatton.org**
❑   Hours: Monday-Friday 9:00am-4:30pm. Saturday-Sunday
        10:00am-4:30pm. Summer weekends and holidays 'til 6:00pm.
        Closed Christmastime and New Years time.
❑   Admission: FREE

A museum of military history of armor and cavalry. You'll see General George S. Patton's personal belongings, a modified Patton jeep, and a Sherman tank. The highlight for kids is probably the American and Foreign armored vehicles and uniforms - how they've changed. Most are displayed outside. The largest tank was never used - why? Military (mini) dioramas (with little army men) depict offensive and defensive strategies.

BUCKLEY WILDLIFE SANCTUARY

1035 Germany Road
(I-64 exit 58, US 60 east, KY 1681, 1650 & 1964),

Frankfort 40601

- ❑ Phone: (859) 873-5711
- ❑ Hours: Wednesday-Friday 9:00am-5:00pm, Saturday & Sunday 9:00am-6:00pm. Closed holidays. Nature Center Building & Gift shop open weekends only 1:00-6:00pm and for special programs. Closed January and February.
- ❑ Admission: $2.00-$3.00 per person. Prices for special events vary.

Observe wildlife at the bird blind, hiking trails, fields, forests and wet areas. Operated by the National Audubon Society, the trails meander along the Kentucky River and bluegrass...havens for birds, mammals and wildflowers.

COUNTRY PLACE JAMBOREE

60 Old Sheeppen Road (off US 60 west)

Frankfort 40601

- ❑ Phone: (502) 223-2359

On any given Saturday night, you'll find a three-hour show that presents the best in traditional country/gospel and bluegrass music or comedy. The concession stand offers home cooking with all the trimmings. A place for the whole family to enjoy and become a "FAMILY AGAIN".

EXECUTIVE MANSION

Capital Avenue building Complex (next to the Capitol building and overlooking the KY River)

Frankfort 40601

- ❑ Phone: (502) 564-8004
  Web: www.state.ky.us/agencies/gov/mansion.htm
- ❑ Hours: Tuesday & Thursday 9:00-11:00am. Also guided tours available by reservation.
- ❑ Admission: FREE

For updates visit our website: www.kidslovepublications.com

Here, sitting in a beautiful setting, is the official Governor's residence. Modeled after Marie Antoinette's summer villa, the rooms you'll see on the tour are the state dining room, ballroom, reception room and formal salon - all rooms designed for "meet and greet" activities.

KENTUCKY HISTORY CENTER

100 West Broadway Street (Downtown)

Frankfort 40601

☐   Phone: (502) 564-1792 or (877) 4-HISTORY

   http://history.ky.gov/Museums/Kentucky_History_Center.htm

☐   Hours: Tuesday-Saturday 10:00am-5:00pm. Closed state holiday weekends

☐   Admission: FREE

☐   Tours: Guided and self-guided.

☐   Miscellaneous: 1792 Museum Store, a world class genealogical research library, changing exhibit gallery.

This large museum includes the most expansive part - the permanent interactive exhibit titled "A Kentucky Journey". Explore 10 distinct time periods in Kentucky history - touching all regions, counties and peoples of the state. Hands-on activities and dioramas include voices and music from that time period. Begin with a lifelike reproduction of the view of the Cumberland Gap. Then, on to: Prehistoric Native Americans hunting in woodlands; Pioneer walk-thru flat boat; Battles of Perryville or the "Houses Divided" in the Civil War; Southern Exposition of 1880 prototypes of very unusual inventions; Simulated Coal Mine; and the Present - George Clooney's scrubs signed by the ER cast, copy of Primetime Live script donated by Diane Sawyer, PapaJohn's Pizza, KFC, Ashland Oil, Corvette and Toyota. There's so much to read and view - all Kentuckians should visit often to learn a little something new each time.

KENTUCKY MILITARY HISTORY MUSEUM

East Main Street at Capital Avenue (Old State Arsenal, US 60)

Frankfort 40601

❑   Phone: (877) 4-HISTORY
    http://history.ky.gov/Museums/Kentucky_Military_History_
    Museum.htm
❑   Hours: Tuesday-Friday 10:00am-5:00pm.
❑   Admission: FREE
❑   Miscellaneous: Daniel Boone's grave is nearby at 215 East Main
    Street (Frankfort Cemetery).

Displays here include a collection of firearms, edged weapons, artillery, uniforms, and flags emphasizing Militia, State Guard, and other volunteer organizations from the Revolution through Operation Desert Storm. Mostly geared towards adults or students studying Kentucky's contributions to US Military. Operated by the Kentucky National Guard.

KENTUCKY STATE CAPITOL AREA

Capital Avenue

Frankfort 40601

❑   Phone: (502) 564-3449
❑   Hours: Monday-Friday 8:00am-4:00pm, Saturday 10:00am-
    2:00pm, Sunday 1:00-4:00pm. Closed major holidays.
❑   Admission: FREE
❑   Tours: Weekdays, guided and self-guided. Weekend tours are
    self-guided.
❑   Miscellaneous: Gift shop, Snack Bar (homemade entrée for
    lunch!)

Completed in 1910, the Beaux Arts design features 70 iconic columns, decorative murals (two of Daniel Boone) and sculptures of Kentucky dignitaries. There is a 212 foot high dome with French influences throughout (Napoleon & Marie Antoinette rooms). Notice all the door knobs bear the state seal. The Floral Clock, located on the West Lawn, is planted with 20,000 colorful flowering plants. The face of this clock is 34 inches in diameter.

It's unique because it's tilted above the reflecting pool supported by its 100 ton planter. Throw a coin into the fountain of the clock and make a wish (coins donated to children's charities). Also, the First Lady Doll Collection, changing history and culture exhibits are featured on the first floor. Oh, by the way, be sure to stop by the Governor's Office and peek in. Maybe they'll offer you a "Govern-mint" as a sweet souvenir of you visit.

KENTUCKY STATE UNIVERSITY
East Main Street
Frankfort 40601

❑   Phone: (502) 567-6000. **Web: www.kysu.edu**
❑   Hours: Monday-Friday 8:00am-4:30pm.
❑   Admission: FREE

KSU is a small, liberal studies university founded in 1886. Visit Jackson Hall with its art gallery and Center for Excellence for the Study of Kentucky African Americans. The Blazer Library is open to the public. Most kids will probably gravitate to the Atwood Agricultural Research Facility and its 166 acre research farm and King Farouk butterfly/moth collection.

KENTUCKY VIETNAM VETERAN'S MEMORIAL
Coffee Tree Road (Off SRKY 676)
Frankfort 40601

❑   Hours: Dawn to dusk
❑   Admission: FREE

Overlooking the city, the names of the Kentuckians who died in Vietnam are etched in granite beneath the giant memorial sundial. The point of the sundial's shadow actually touches the veteran's name on the anniversary of his death!... Incredible! Recognized as one of the most original and unusual memorials in the nation, it is truly touching.

LESLIE MORRIS PARK ON FORT HILL

300 Broadway (Old Capitol Annex)

Frankfort 40601

- ❑ Phone: (800) 960-7200
- ❑ Hours: Daylight hours. Visitors Center: Tuesday, Thursday & Saturday 11:00am-4:00pm.
- ❑ Admission: FREE
- ❑ Tours: self guided tours begin at Fort Hill Visitors Center located on the 1st floor of the Annex.
- ❑ Miscellaneous: No restroom facilities on Fort Hill.

This Civil War site is where local militia held off an attack by Confederate cavalrymen attempting to invade and destroy the capitol of Kentucky. The walls of Fort Boone still stand, as do the earthworks of a second fort known as the New Redoubt. The walking tour points out the 1864 skirmish site.

LT. GOVERNOR'S MANSION

420 High Street

Frankfort 40601

- ❑ Phone: (502) 564-3449. **Web: www.state.ky.us**
- ❑ Hours: Tuesday & Thursday 1:30-3:30pm. Guided tours offered by appointment
- ❑ Admission: FREE

This is the oldest official U.S. executive residence still in use. The federal style mansion was home to 33 Kentucky governors from 1798-1914. Now the official residence of the Lt. Governor, the first floor is available to tour. Much of the focus of the tour is mention of seven U.S. presidents who visited and why.

OLD STATE CAPITOL

Broadway and Lewis Street

Frankfort 40601

- ❑ Phone: (502) 564-3016
- **Web: www.kyhistory.org/Museums/Old_state_Capitol.htm**

❑   Hours: Tuesday-Friday 10:00am-5:00pm. Closed New Years, Easter, Thanksgiving, and Christmastime.

❑   Admission: FREE

❑   Tours: Guided tours are available by appointment.

This national landmark, operated by the Kentucky Historical Society, was the seat of government from 1830 to 1910. The most interesting part of the structure is the unique, self-supporting staircase held together by pressure of the circular angles. This was the only pro-Union state capitol occupied by the Confederate army during the Civil War and, in 1900, for a time, the place where Kentuckians threatened to fight their own miniature civil war.

REBECCA-RUTH CANDY

112 East Second Street (Downtown & Capital Avenue (near Kentucky River)

Frankfort 40601

❑   Phone: (502) 223-7475 or (800) 444-3766

   Web: www.rebeccaruth.com

❑   Admission: FREE

❑   Tours: Monday-Saturday 9:00am-4:30pm (Best times are before 1:00pm). (January-November). 10 minutes, guided.

This candy store business was co-founded in 1919 by two schoolteachers, Rebecca and Ruth. They started in their houses making candy over the holidays. Today Ruth Booe's grandson is owner and hands-on operator of this confectionery (you'll probably bump into him). The highlights include free samples, an educational video, antique cooking furnace with hand-stirred copper kettles, production areas and "Edna's Table". A 12 foot curved marble slab was purchased by Ruth for $10 in 1917, now it's named after Edna, an employee of 67 years (ate candy 'til the day she died). They make 100 varieties of confections including some unique to Kentucky at 1000 pounds/day. Cute, small-town, casual way to spend a few minutes in a candy factory - what fun!

SALATO WILDLIFE EDUCATION CENTER

#1 Game Farm Road (I-64 exit 53B to US 127N to US 60)

Frankfort 40601

❑ Phone: (502) 564-7863 or (800) 858-1549
   Web: www.kdfwr.state.ky.us/salato1.htm
❑ Hours: Tuesday-Friday 9:00am-5:30pm, Saturday 10:00am-
   6:00pm, Sunday 1:00-6:00pm (May-September). Tuesday-
   Saturday 10:00am-5:00pm, Sunday 1:00-5:00pm (October-
   April). Park open sunrise to sunset. Closed most holidays. Open
   Memorial Day, July 4th, and Labor Day.
❑ Admission: FREE
❑ Miscellaneous: 132 acre complex with public fishing, picnicking
   and wildlife viewing. Kentucky Afield Gift Shop.

This educational center has interactive and interpretive exhibits
featuring native Kentucky plants and animals. Wonderfully run by
the Department of Wildlife and Fishing, they keep it simple but,
naturally modern. Begin your viewing with stories told by a
Native American girl in the mural called Kentuckians Before
Boone. Next, you'll gander at warm-water fish like Bass, Bluegill
and Catfish. Around the corner view Kentucky Record Fish
mounted on a giant board with storyboards that tell cute tales of the
"Big Catch". Just around the bend is the most unique site - have
you ever seen a live Alligator Snapping Turtle? It was amazing to
watch this prehistoric creature perform for us - the combination of
claws, scales and turtle shell will catch your attention for sure!
Outdoors in several different, easily accessible areas, take a look at
live American Bald Eagles, white-tailed deer with wild turkeys,
bison and elk or the new bobcat or black bear exhibit. Further out
on the trail is Dragonfly Marsh observation wetland. What can
you find?

VEST-LINDSEY HOUSE

401 Wapping Street
(downtown outskirts, near Rebecca-Ruth Candy)

Frankfort 40601

❑   Phone: (502) 564-6980

   Web: www.state.ky.us/agencies/finance/attract/vestlin.htm

❑   Hours: Monday-Friday 9:00am-4:00pm

❑   Admission: FREE

❑   Miscellaneous: State Meeting House for government agencies.
    You might catch VIP's floating around.

The early 19th century Federal House was the boyhood home of US Senator George Graham Vest. He was a famous trial lawyer, mostly remembered for his "Tribute to the Dog" speech, from which is coined the phrase "dog is man's best friend". He was defending a man whose dog had killed a neighbor's sheep. Of special interest to kids is the floor cloth in the dining areas (vs. carpet). It was the forerunner of linoleum. Also, kids can help demo the dumb-waiter used to serve from the downstairs kitchen. Be sure to pick up a copy of Vest's famous speech before you leave.

CREASEY MAHAN NATURE PRESERVE

12501 Harmony Landing Road (Gene Snyder Freeway exit 9B)

Goshen 40026

❑   Phone: (502) 228-4362

Hike the wooded trails, discover wildlife or just picnic with the family at this year-round park (open daylight hours). More than 5 miles of nature trails, 15 minutes to 2 hours in duration, wind through the preserve. Special places like the Wetlands, the Meadows, the Frog Pond, and the Rock Platform are favorite "outdoor labs" for students. The Nature Center highlights lifelike dioramas featuring foxes, deer, wild turkeys, birds, frogs and some Native American history.

DANIEL BOONE, THE MAN & THE LEGEND

West Lexington Street (Fort Harrod State Park, outdoors behind the
park in Amphitheater), **Harrodsburg** 40330

- ❑   Phone: (800) 85-BOONE. **Web: www.boonedrama.com**
- ❑   Hours: Tuesday-Saturday (early June thru mid-August),
       Showtime is 8:30pm, Sunday 7:00pm. Approx. 2 hour show with
       intermission.
- ❑   Admission: $12.00 adult, $10.00 senior, $8.00 child (12 and
       under). Sunday tickets are $8.00 for everyone.
- ❑   Miscellaneous: Add a $2.00 ticket includes admission to Old Fort
       Harrod State Park (valid after 5:00pm, same day as performance)
       except Sundays. The amphitheatre is set with chairs (not benches)
       as seats.

As the kids adorn their new coon-skin hat, learn the "inside story"
of Daniel Boone's dreams and disappointments - get inside his
head - what drove him? A storyteller shares with you Kentucky's
Frontier Adventure - a professionally acted outdoor drama. It
definitely relives the action-packed exploration, danger and
romance of Boone's exploration and settlement of a new land
through the Cumberland Gap. Explosions of excitement burst on
stage as you sense the dynamics between the enticement of lush
land and game versus the sacred hunting ground of the Shawnee
Indians. This land "Kanta-Ke" they planned to protect from all
intruders. The play ends with the fiery defense of the fort against a
full-scale Indian attack. Everyone concluded that this is truly the
best way to learn frontiersmen's amazing challenges. The best
way to appreciate a hero's life! You even get to meet and greet the
actors afterwards - have them sign your program or Boone cap.

DIXIE BELLE RIVERBOAT

3501 Lexington Road (Shaker Village of Pleasant Hill, US 68E)

Harrodsburg 40330

- ❑   Phone: (859) 734-5411 or (800) 734-5611
       Web: www.shakervillageky.org
- ❑   Admission: $5.00 (age 6+).

❑   Tours: Every 2 hours beginning at Noon (late April-October).

The 150-passenger riverboat leaves Shaker Landing, the site where Shakers loaded flatboats with goods headed for Southern markets. Narrated excursions go through Kentucky River Palisades complete with limestone canyon, sparkling waterfalls and a close-up of river flora and fauna.

OLD FORT HARROD STATE PARK

South College Street (US 68, SW of Lexington, near US 127 south)

Harrodsburg 40330

❑   Phone: (859) 734-3314. Web: www.oldfortharrod.com

❑   Hours: Fort: 8:30am-5:00pm (mid-March - October). 8:00am-4:30pm (November-early March). Open 'til Legend of Daniel Boone show begins, summer. Museum: 9:00am-5:30pm. (mid-March - November). Closed Thanksgiving, Christmas week to New Years and weekends, December-February.

❑   Admission: $2.00-$4.00 per person.

❑   Miscellaneous: Gift Shop, picnicking, animal corral (some petting). Miscellaneous: Gift shop, picnicking, animal corral (some petting)

In 1774, Captain James Harrod established the first permanent settlement west of the Alleghenies in the hills of what would become central Kentucky. The reconstructed fort was built near the original. Costumed craftspeople perform pioneer tasks such as broom-making, wood-working, basketry, waving, farming, gardening, blacksmithing and woodworking. The folks even sell their wares in their shops/homes - purchase one as a souvenir. Interact by trying to do some pioneer chores (like dyeing yarn or cooking stew). The most unique spot has to be the frontier schoolhouse. With dirt floors and a pretty schoolteacher you'll learn to use a "hornbook". This is a school slate made of wood with a "laminate" surface made from cow horn chips. The teacher writes the lesson using charcoal and each child holds their "book" in front of them to recite their lessons. And your kids think they have it rough!

ABRAHAM LINCOLN BIRTHPLACE
NATIONAL HISTORIC SITE

2995 Lincoln Farm Road
(I-65 exit 91, follow KY 61 south to US 31E)

Hodgenville 42748

❏   Phone: (270) 358-3137. **Web: www.nps.gov/abli**
❏   Hours: Memorial Day-Labor Day 8:00am-6:45pm. Rest of year
      8:00am-4:45pm. Closed Thanksgiving, Christmas & New Years.
      Eastern Time.
❏   Admission: Donations.
❏   Miscellaneous: Picnicking, Hiking. A boardwalk ramp trail is
      available for strollers and wheelchairs. Near the steps is Sinking
      Spring used by the family and the 400 year old "boundary" oak
      tree.

A granite memorial with 56 steps, 30 foot wide, leads to the shrine
(the steps signify the number of years of Lincoln's life). Enclosed
inside is a log cabin which is the symbolic birthplace of Abraham
Lincoln (1809-1865). The Visitor Center houses exhibits on the
Lincoln family and a video program on Lincoln's boyhood
(humbly produced, as Mr. Lincoln would have wanted it). Our
family's highlight was seeing the actual Lincoln family Bible (with
study notes written by Lincoln family members)!

LINCOLN JAMBOREE

2579 Lincoln Farm Road

Hodgenville 42748

❏   Phone: (270) 358-3545. **Web: www.lincolnjamboree.com**
❏   Hours: Every Saturday night, usually at 8:00pm.
❏   Admission: $8.00 per person, reserved seating.

A well-known country music showplace with family shows since
1954. Country restaurant on premises. A Family Show -
Absolutely No Drinking.

For updates visit our website: www.kidslovepublications.com

LINCOLN MUSEUM

66 Lincoln Square (downtown, town square - look for the bronze
Lincoln statue)

Hodgenville 42748

❏   Phone: (270) 358-3163.   **Web: www.lincolnmuseumky.org**
❏   Hours: Monday-Saturday 8:30am-4:30pm, Sunday 12:30-
4:30pm.
❏   Admission: $3.00 adult, $2.50 senior (60+), $1.50 child (5-12).

This two-story museum houses 12 wax figure authentic scenes of
great significance in Lincoln's life and our nation's history. The
first scene is titled "The Cabin Years" (from local boyhood home)
and the last scene #12 is "Ford's Theatre". The 18 minute film
shown upstairs is another way to see Lincoln's phases of life.
Unlike most wax museums, this one is well lit, not frightening to
the younger kids. The scenes are enlightened by the descriptions in
the brochure you receive upon paid admission. Well done!

LINCOLN'S BOYHOOD HOME

Knob Creek Farm (US 31E northeast)

Hodgenville 42748

❏   Phone: (270) 358-3137 Park Headquarters.
❏   Hours: Summers 10:00am-6:00pm. Fall/Spring 10:00am-5:00pm.
Daily April-October.
❏   Admission: up to $1.00 per person.
❏   Miscellaneous: Now operated by NPS, affiliated with Abraham
Lincoln Birthplace.

"My earliest recollection is of the Knob Creek Place" says Mr.
Lincoln. Abraham (at two years old) and his parents and sister
Sarah lived here from 1811-1816. Here he learned to talk and later
recalled memories of childhood here: a field to pick berries; the
baby brother who was born and died here; staying by his mother's
side and watching her face while listening to her read her bible;
short periods of subscription school (he called it "blab" school
because you recited lessons all day long); and falling in the
swollen Knob Creek while playing on a footlog. It was here where

a young boy Lincoln first saw slaves transported along the road in front of his home. You can take a look inside the cabin and read the giant storyboard. You can also call ahead for a guided tour (school groups get a great study bag to use for further study back home). You'll surely appreciate Abraham's poor beginnings - yet be inspired by the accomplishments of a man who didn't come from affluent means.

OLDHAM COUNTY HISTORY CENTER

106 North Second Avenue

La Grange 40031

- ❑ Phone: (502) 222-0826
  Web: www.oldhamcountyhistoricalsociety.org
- ❑ Hours: Tuesday-Saturday 1:00-4:00pm.
- ❑ Admission: $2.00-$4.00 (age 6+).

The county has put together a facility with changing exhibits and programs that chronicle the development and history of the area. There's also an outdoor sculpture.

BELLE OF LOUISVILLE & SPIRIT OF JEFFERSON

(Fourth Street Wharf. I-64 west to Third St. exit, left onto River Rd., right at Second St.)

Louisville 40202

- ❑ Phone: (502) 574-2355 or (866) 832-0011
  Web: www.belleoflouisville.org
- ❑ Admission: $12.00 adult, $9.00 senior (60+), $6.00 child (3-12)
- ❑ Tours: Belle Sightseeing Cruise, (Memorial Day weekend-Labor Day). Board at 11:30am or Noon and cruise for two hours shortly after that, Tuesday-Sunday. Spirit of Jefferson kid-friendly, historical cruises include the Locks Tour (constructed early 1960's, is over 8600 ft. long and has 9 gates, 22 ft. by 100ft.- best way to see is by boat) and the Riverside Cruise every weekend in summer plus Saturdays in Sept. and Oct. (includes tour of historic Farnsley-Moremen home).

❑   Miscellaneous: Spirit of Jefferson is charming with more modern updates and usually is used for weekday cruises. Both boats have a café, concessions, gift shops and restrooms.

The World's Greatest Steamboat was built in 1914 as the "Idlewild" hauling cargo and people on the Mississippi River. In the mid-1940's she was renamed "Avalon" and began "tramping" (steamboats used for traveling from one town to another for business transport and shows). As the Avalon, she became the most widely traveled steamer in US history. It is now a National Landmark. Almost 200 feet long and 46 feet wide, she is powered by two steam engines (one port, one starboard) and has three decks with the capacity to carry 800 people. The steam calliope, powered by steam from the engine room, has 32 whistles and a sweet Showboat sound. Be sure to check out the original photos of personnel and similar vessels. While walking thru the gallery, you'll also be able to chat with the captain and shipmates. You'll hear talk of the olden days and special points of interest like the Falls of the Ohio fossil bed, Muhammad Ali center, and famous bridges and shipyards. Unique to this historical sightseeing tour was the impressive tie-in of a historical steamboat character sharing stories - we'd not seen that before! Also, the captain, engineers and 1st mates were very accessible and happy to sit and spend time answering questions. NOTE: The narration is key to a good tour. If you can't hear, move closer to a speaker.

JOE & MIKE'S PRETTY GOOD TOURS
(depart from local hotels)
Louisville 40202

❑   Phone: (502) 459-1247
❑   Admission: $20.00 adult, $10.00 child (5-10).
❑   Tours: Tours depart major area hotels twice daily. Three hour tours in 14-person mini-bus. Closed New Years, Easter, Thanksgiving and Christmas.

Main Street has the second-largest collection of cast-iron storefronts in the United States; the largest exposed Devonian fossil beds on the continent are at the Falls of the Ohio. These are

among the better-known bits of local trivia served up during one of
Joe & Mike's Pretty Good Tours, as one of the owners drives past
historic Louisville landmarks, pointing out places to eat, shop and
sample history.

LITTLE LOOM HOUSE

328 Kenwood Hill Road

Louisville 40202

- ❑ Phone: (502) 367-4792
- ❑ Hours: Tuesday, Wednesday & the 3rd Saturday of the month
  10:00am-3:00pm. Closed Thanksgiving and Christmas-New
  Years.
- ❑ Admission: $3.00 (ages 2+)

Tours, demonstrations, classes on spinning and weaving to persons
of all ages. They are devoted to keeping the art of hand-weaving
and its history alive. The Loom House is housed in three century-
old cabins. A gift shop is on the premises.

LOUISVILLE BALLET

315 East Main Street (performances at the KY Center for the Arts, 5 Riverfront Plaza)

Louisville 40202

- ❑ Phone: (502) 583-3150 or 584-7777 tickets
  Web: www.louisvilleballet.org

The State Ballet of Kentucky performs classics like "The
Nutcracker", "Swan Lake" and many children's classics.

LOUISVILLE SCIENCE CENTER

727 West Main Street (Downtown, I-64 exit 4)

Louisville 40202

- ❑ Phone: (800) 591-2203. **Web: www.louisvillescience.org**
- ❑ Hours: Monday-Saturday 9:30am-5:00pm (also Friday-Saturday
  evening until 9:00pm), Sunday Noon-6:00pm; closed
  Thanksgiving and Christmas.

For updates visit our website: www.kidslovepublications.com

❏   Admission: $8.50 adult, $7.50 senior (60+) and child (2-12). Combo tickets w/ IMAX theatre approx. $2.00 more per person.

❏   Miscellaneous: KIDZONE has 45 minute ticket (by request only) times every hour except Tuesday and Saturday mornings (members only then). IMAX Theatre with many daily showtimes. Galaxy Bistro.

As you enter the brightly-colored 40,000 square feet of hands-on science, you might first notice the "Be-in-a-Bubble" or "Bubble Scope" exhibits. Areas covered in the museum include Space Exploration, Egyptian Culture, Natural History and Health. But, our favorite floor has to be the second floor where "The World We Create" and KIDZONE can be found. KIDZONE is for the younger set (age 7 and under) with their adults. Initially, you may sit back and watch the kiddies play "Splash" (water play) or even "Let's Build" (construction toys, blocks, pulleys and conveyors). However, when you get to "Hop On" or "Take Off" play, the whole family is dressing up and playing pretend. Be a bus, ambulance or plane driver or passenger using apparatus from real vehicles and airplanes. A giant "'Thumbs Up'" to the designers of this giant play equipment! Youngsters can apply what they learned by tagging along with older siblings in the "World We Create" (get an Early Learners Guide from KIDZONE). Now you follow inventions (many created by Kentuckians) like Building Homes, Wind Tunnels, Map Master (find your house), Toppling Towers or Shake, Rattle and Roll (test structures you create with blocks). The World Within Us allows you to tour the human body and check your senses, one at a time. As they say here – "SCIENTISTS AT PLAY"!

LOUISVILLE SLUGGER MUSEUM

800 West Main Street (Eighth and Main, downtown. I-64 West or I-65 South, exit Third Street), Louisville 40202

❏   Phone: (502) 588-7228. **Web: www.sluggermuseum.org**

❏   Hours: Monday-Saturday 9:00am-5:00pm, Sunday Noon-5:00pm (Sundays April-October).

❏   Admission $6.00 adult, $5.00 senior (60+) $3.50 child (6-12).

❏   Tours: Last Tour begins 1 hour before closing. No bat production on Sundays & Holidays.

❑ Miscellaneous: Be sure to take the tour - everyone gets a small souvenir bat to take home.

You can't miss the entrance to this place - outside or inside. The world's largest baseball bat (120 foot, 68 thousand pounds of steel) rests against the outside wall of the manufacturing plant and the "Let's Play Ball" ball and glove sculpture is the heaviest such structure. Both are great photo ops. See and touch the actual bats swung by legendary sluggers like Hank Aaron, Babe Ruth (thicker at the end), Ty Cobb and Ken Griffey, Jr. (lighter). Begin with a video called "The Heart of the Game" that emotionally pays tribute to that magical moment in sports when we hear the crack of the bat. Now that you're in the mood, go through an underground locker room and dugout and onto the field. After the umpire (guide) explains the rules, he shouts "Play Ball" and the group scatters for pictures, "Chats" with bat boys, and glances at memorabilia from great moments and players. Experience the sensation of a 90 mph pitch coming right at you at the great "Batter Up" famous pitchers display! By the time you've taken another good look at an actual Babe Ruth Home Run bat (see the marks on the bat – each one for a home run!), you'll walk thru a replica Northwest White Ash Forest as you move onto the Hillerich & Bradsby Co. factory. See modern bats made from a round wooden cylinder. They are formed from one pass thru a special lathe and then branded with the Louisville Slugger logo and player's name. This is a great All American place for the whole family!

STAGE ONE, THE LOUISVILLE CHILDRENS THEATRE

501 West Main Street (performances at the KY Center for the Arts)

Louisville 40202

❑ Phone: (502) 589-5946 or (800) 989-5946. www.stageone.org

Their focus is strictly on productions for children and families both at public performances and school outreach programs. Shows like "Huck Finn", "The Velveteen Rabbit", and contemporary Christmas themes like "A Winnie-the-Pooh Christmas" are likely each season. Season runs September-May.

For updates visit our website: www.kidslovepublications.com

THOMAS EDISON HOUSE

729-31 East Washington Street (I-65N to Brook St. exit to Market
St., turn right and go east to left on Clay St. to E. Washington St)

Louisville 40202

❑   Phone: (502) 585-5247. **Web: www.edisonhouse.org**
❑   Hours: Tuesday-Saturday 10:00am-2:00pm. Closed New Years,
Derby Day, July 4, Thanksgiving, and Christmas Eve/Day.
❑   Admission: $4.00 adult, $3.00 senior (60+), $2.00 child (6-17).

Although you may think - why take the time to visit a place Edison
lived at for only a brief time? Well, we highly recommend you
don't have the same regrets as the boss that fired Thomas Edison -
the reason he left Louisville. The guides here will highlight many
points of the famous inventor's life including working on the
railroad, learning Morse Code (try it yourself in his room) to being
fired and turning out his first invention, the stock ticker. A great
video describes the inventor's life. Did you know he actually
started General Electric? Some of his 1093 patents are on display
including: early motion pictures (the first one was of a man
sneezing!), phonograph, dictating machines, and a collection of
electric light bulbs. They have cute light bulb souvenirs to chose
from and a picture of our favorite invention - the Power Nap! You
have to go just to get the scoop on that!

LOUISVILLE STONEWARE COMPANY

731 Brent Street (I-65 off Broadway Street exit east to Barret
Street, turn right), **Louisville** 40204

❑   Phone: (502) 582-1900 or (800) 626-1800
Web: www.louisvillestoneware.com
❑   Hours: Monday-Saturday 9:00am-6:00pm. Sunday, Noon-
5:00pm.
❑   Admission: $5.00 (age 12+)
❑   Tours: Monday-Friday at 10:30am and 1:30pm. 35-40 minutes.
❑   Miscellaneous: Paint your own pottery workshop - pay by the
item - excellent way to end tour (make pre-arrangements with 5
or more).

Louisville Stoneware Company (cont.)

Nationally famous hand-painted pottery (dinnerware, ovenware, giftware) since 1879. On tour, see the entire process. Begin at the Raw Clay Storage Bin where mounds of dry clay are stacked as tall as your garage. They next mix raw clay with water, take out air bubbles and finally extrude clay fit for the potter's wheel. Unusually shaped pieces (like birdhouses) are cast upstairs. You'll see the jigger production pieces created on a potters wheel with molds and the potter's special trained touch. The handles are all hand formed by two quiet, artistic women. There's a large room full of women painting trains, fish, Noah's Ark, etc. on the wares. You next see the pieces dipped and set to dry in kilns. Note: We think the best souvenirs of all are those hand-made, especially by your kids. For around $12.00 your kids can create their own design on pottery made here. What a wonderful way to have kids apply what they just saw being made to their own creation!

AMERICAN PRINTING HOUSE FOR THE BLIND

1839 Frankfort Avenue (I-64 and US 42 east)

Louisville 40206

❑   Phone: (502) 895-2405 or (800) 223-1839. **Web: www.aph.org**

❑   Hours: Museum: Monday-Friday 8:30am-4:30pm. Closed holidays.

❑   Admission: FREE

❑   Tours: Monday-Thursday at 10:00am and 2:00pm. Make reservations for groups of 10 or more. Suggested age for touring is age 9 years and up. Tour takes one hour.

Browse through a Braille magazine as you wait for your tour to begin. Founded in 1858, this place is one of the world's largest and oldest printing companies creating products for the visually-impaired. You'll start in the hands-on area (our favorite part - truly fascinating - really!) where visitors can actually learn some of the Braille alphabet, read a popular book in both Braille and written word, or test a talking color analyzer that helps the color-blind match their clothing. Try your math skills with multiplication cards for the blind. Next, briefly tour the plant where they print, bind and proofread all kinds of books and magazines. The museum displays embossed books, early mechanical Braille writers and tactile maps and globes. This is also where you take home a hand-made souvenir of you name typed in Braille. A truly curious, enchanting place! Could you guess what would possibly be their largest Braille project ever? - The World Book Encyclopedia - 145 volumes (see it!).

HADLEY POTTERY

1570 Story Avenue
(halfway between Amer. Printing & Edison's Home)

Louisville 40206

❑   Phone: (502) 584-2171. **Web: www.hadleypottery.com**
❑   Hours: Store hours are Monday-Friday from 8:30am-5:00pm. Eastern time and Saturday from 9:00am-1:00pm. Saturday hours are extended from the second week in November until Christmas.
❑   Admission: FREE
❑   Tours: Monday-Friday at 2:00pm (except in the summer when the temp. is over 85 degrees). No age restrictions; however, small children and elderly or handicapped will not be able to easily manage the very steep staircase to the basement where most of the activity occurs. Some young children feel the basement is also dark and scary.

Pottery by Mary Alice Hadley has an international reputation and is known for its whimsical designs of clay stoneware. They use a process (you will see during the tour) called "underglaze decoration". The pottery is fired only one time; and this single fire process produces ware with a maximum bond between the body, decoration and glaze, with the result that the decoration is as permanent as the piece. In ware produced by the alternate process of separate firings for the body, glaze and decoration (as is the practice with most dinnerware), the decoration (and sometimes the glaze) is readily subject to abrasion and the chemical action of strong cleaning solutions and to crazing. The high temperature limits the range of colors that can be used in applying decoration. Colors adaptable for use with the white over-glaze are blue, green and rust, with blue-black and yellow available under special circumstances. You'll see artisans hand-painting with these colors on the second floor. Most children like the painting area best.

JOSEPH A. CALLOWAY ARCHAEOLOGICAL MUSEUM

2825 Lexington Road (Southern Baptist Theological Seminary)

Louisville 40206

❑   Phone: (502) 897-4141

❑   Hours: Monday-Friday 8:00am-5:00pm, Saturday 9:00am-5:00pm.

Billy Graham's archives, a copy of the Rosetta Stone and a 2,700 year-old mummy are featured in this collection of ancient Near Eastern and Egyptian artifacts.

LOCUST GROVE HISTORIC HOME

561 Blankenbaker Lane (I-264 exit 22, US 42 west or I-71 exit 2, follow signs), **Louisville** 40207

❑   Phone: (502) 897-9845. **Web: www.locustgrove.org**

❑   Hours: Monday-Saturday 10:00am-4:30pm, Sunday 1:30-4:30pm. Hands-on History open Tuesday-Saturday 11:00am-3:00pm, June-August. Closed New Years, Easter, Derby Day, Thanksgiving, and Christmas.

❑   Admission: $6.00 adult, $5.00 senior (60+), $3.00 child (6-12). $2.00 extra per child for Hands-on History.

❑   Tours: Monday-Saturday at 10:15, 11:15am, 12:15pm, 1:30pm, 2:30pm and 3:30pm.

❑   Miscellaneous: Pioneer Days or Woodworking Camp available in summer. Gift Shop. Video about history of site shown in visitor's center.

The retirement home (beginning in 1809) of George Rogers Clark - a frontiersman and Revolutionary War General. The mansion, garden and nine outbuildings are furnished in period. Start in the parlor room where such guests as Presidents James Monroe, Zachary Taylor or Andrew Jackson were greeted. Also Lewis & Clark (William) visited and stored artifacts from exhibitions in the ballroom upstairs. In the Dining Room, you'll find out why sugar was kept in large cabinets under lock & key. Why was the letter "J" missing from the alphabet in pioneer days? Did you know settlers (pre Civil War) wore shoes with no left or right foot distinction? The Hands-On History Cabin is highly recommended (summer only). This log cabin is where children can try on clothing reproductions and sort through the contents of a Revolutionary War soldier's trunk. Kids can also try quilting, weaving, pioneer games, carding wool, surveying and mapping a new city or writing with a real quill pen. Photos in this area make wonderful souvenirs - great learning too.

KENTUCKY DERBY MUSEUM AND CHURCHILL DOWNS

704 Central Avenue (I-264 & Taylor Blvd., Follow signs)

Louisville 40208

❑ Phone: (502) 637-1111or (502) 637-7097

Web: www.derbymuseum.org

❑ Hours: Monday-Saturday 9:00am-5:00pm, Sunday, Noon-5:00pm. Closed Oaks and Derby days (first Friday/Saturday in May), Thanksgiving and Christmas.

❑ Admission: $8.00 adult, $7.00 senior (55+), $3.00 child (5-12)

❑ Miscellaneous: Finish Line Shop, Derby Café (lunch). Half hour walking tour of Churchill Downs (weather permitting, extra $6.00 per person).

Although the actual Derby Day and Churchill Downs races may not be appropriate for the young kids, the Museum and Tour of Churchill Downs is fun for the family. The museum has 3 floors of displays that showcase thoroughbred racing in the Derby - the greatest two minutes in sports. Different areas focus on: The Horses (owners and trainers, too), The Jockeys and Derby Day. The 360 degree audiovisual recreation is a must see. Located in the center of the first floor, the circular theatre really captures the "feeling" of all people involved. Other highlights are the Starting Gate (you walk thru one as you enter the museum); "Weigh in Please" exhibit where you weigh yourself the day of the race and compare your weight to an average jockey (they average 126 pounds). Finally, our favorite, "Riders Up" - try riding like a jockey on a horse in position to win the race. Don't sit down on the saddle - you'll lose the race!

SPEED ART MUSEUM

2035 South Third Street (exit I-65 to St. Catherine, Arthur St. or Eastern Parkway - adjacent to the Univ. of Louisville)

Louisville 40208

❑   Phone: (502) 634-2700. **Web: www.speedmuseum.org**
❑   Hours: Tuesday, Wednesday & Friday 10:30am-4:00pm, Thursday 10:30am-8:00pm, Saturday 10:30am-5:00pm and Sunday Noon-5:00pm.
❑   Admission: $3.50 ages 2+ to Art Sparks. Admission to the Speed's Permanent Collection is FREE (donation is appreciated).
❑   Miscellaneous: Café Bristol open for lunch Tuesday-Saturday. Gift shop.

Although a planned group tour of any significant art museum is a wonderful cultural experience for children, the Art Sparks Interactive Gallery inside this museum makes this art museum the best for kids. Don a Dutch collar and cape and play Rembrandt, dance inside a video artwork, build scale models of downtown skylines, or turn your picture into pop art. In the Electronic Art Room, young visitors can create digital art while visiting museums around the world via the Internet. If you venture, as a family, into the "grown-up" galleries be sure to get a Gallery Pack, a kid-size bag filled with puzzles, seek-and-find, and other hand-outs that take "boring" out of the kid's vocabulary.

PORTLAND MUSEUM

2308 Portland Avenue

Louisville 40212

❑   Phone: (502) 776-7678

❑   Hours: Tuesday-Friday 10:00am-4:30pm

❑   Admission: $2.00 adult, $1.50 senior and student.

Do newsreels of the 1937 flood or a terrain model of the Falls of the Ohio fossil bed interest you? Study 19th century times (when the town was a thriving river port) through dioramas and mannequins titled "Portland: the Land, the River and the People". The museum is housed in Beech Grove, built in 1852 as a country estate. It also features a 23 minute historical light & sound show.

LOUISVILLE ZOO

1100 Trevilian Way (I-264 exit 14)

Louisville 40213

❑   Phone: (502) 459-2181. **Web: www.louisvillezoo.org**

❑   Hours: Daily 10:00am-5:00pm (April-Labor Day); open 'til 4:00pm rest of year. Closed New Years, Thanksgiving and Christmas. Last entrance is one hour before closing.

❑   Admission: $9.95 adult, $7.95 senior (60+), $6.95 child (3-11).

❑   Miscellaneous: Mini-train ride circling zoo. Picnicking spots. Cafes. Carousel rides. Roarchestra - summertime Louisville orchestra concert series on the lawn.

The Mammal and bird exhibits here are arranged by geographic regions. One of the largest arachnid (spiders, centipedes) exhibits is here and it's the only one like it in the U.S. The Islands Pavilion, Indonesian Village is home to tigers and orangutans; there's a walk-thru aviary; the Aquarium has a rainforest, reptiles and fish; the petting zoo features African farm animals; and the MetaZoo Education Center provides amphibian exhibits and microscopes through which small creatures can be viewed. The Gorilla Forest and the Australian Outback include a lot of close looks back from the animals.

MUSIC THEATRE LOUISVILLE

1080 Amphitheater Road (performances at Iroquois Amphitheater, I-264 to Southern Pkwy, south to New Cut Rd east, right on Kenwood), **Louisville** 40214

❑   Phone: (502) 589-4060 or (502) 361-3100 tickets
     Web: www.musictheatrelouisville.com
❑   Hours: Thursday-Saturday 8:30pm, Sunday 7:30pm (late June-August).
❑   Admission: Ranges from $12.00-$18.00

Professional musicals presented under the stars at Iroquois Park Amphitheater with productions like "Annie" or the "Wizard of Oz".

SONS OF THE AMERICAN REVOLUTION HISTORICAL MUSEUM

1000 South Fourth Street

Louisville 40216

❑   Phone: (502) 589-1776
❑   Hours: Monday-Friday 9:30am-4:30pm
❑   Admission: FREE

The national headquarters of the Sons of the American Revolution Historical Museum features a continuing program of acquisitions for display, ranging from objects related to the U.S. as it emerged as a new nation to artifacts of the Revolutionary War and Early American decorative arts. Look for the flag from the War of 1812 and a life-size replica of the Liberty Bell from the original's manufacturer.

LOUISVILLE MOTOR SPEEDWAY

1900 Outer Loop (I-65 exit 127)

Louisville 40219

❑   Phone: (502) 966-2277
❑   Hours: Friday & Saturday at around 7:00pm (April-September)
❑   Admission charged.

The speedway features NASCAR sanctioned racing on a 3/8 mile asphalt oval track with a figure-8 design.

For updates visit our website: www.kidslovepublications.com

HAWKS VIEW GLASS BLOWING GALLERY

170 Carter Avenue
(I-65 exit 121 E to Bluelick Road North to Carter Avenue)

Louisville 40229

❑ Phone: (502) 955-1010
❑ Hours: Monday-Saturday 10:00am-5:00pm.
❑ Admission: FREE
❑ Tours: Daily, groups must have appointments. Best to call ahead
for best viewing times each week.

Tour this facility and watch artists create small and large unusually shaped glass blown art. Although the thought of gift glass art may not appeal to parents with young children (to display in their home), the idea of purchases as gifts will certainly appeal to you more after watching something being created. Try to figure out which shape they're forming before they finish (there's a good chance it may be something with fins or feathers).

LOUISVILLE RIVER BATS

401 East Main Street (Louisville Slugger Field)

Louisville 40233

❑ Phone: (502) 367-9121. **Web: www.batsbaseball.com**
❑ Season: April-September

AAA professional baseball farm club for the Cincinnati Reds. Tickets run $4.00-$8.00.

SIX FLAGS KENTUCKY KINGDOM

937 Phillips Lane - KY Fair Expo Center (I-65 & 1-264)

Louisville 40241

❑ Phone: (502) 366-2231 or (800) SCREAMS
Web: www.sixflags.com/kentuckykingdom
❑ Hours: Open daily June-August beginning at 10:00am or
11:00am until dark; Weekends only in April, May, September
and October. Hours vary during the Kentucky State Fair from
mid-to-late August. Hurricane Bay open daily 11:00am-7:00pm,
Memorial Day - late September (weather permitting).

❑　Admission: General approx. $37.00. Senior (55+) and kids under 48 inches tall are approx. half price. Seniors (65+) and children (3 and under) are FREE. Additional fee for dragsters and during the Kentucky State Fair. Parking $4.00.

Young ones will love the Looney Tunes character shows, the sing-along musical shows and the special areas with kiddie rides. The older children will gravitate towards the virtual reality ride, a 16-story free-fall ride, and the world's longest stand-up coaster (plus 7 other coasters!). The whole family will have fun at Hurricane Bay waterpark (included in admission). With a 750,000 gallon wave pool, giant waterslides, water tubing and kiddie areas – this is a great way to cool off. There's also a newer family roller coaster where every ride car is individual so you always feel like the "lead" car (this coaster is not as steep and a great way to "graduate" from the kiddie rides). Food, games and traditional rides are offered throughout the park and changing areas are available in Hurricane Bay.

TOM SAWYER, E.P. STATE PARK

3000 Freys Hill Road (Gene Snyder Freeway northeast to westbound Westport Road exit)

Louisville 40241

❑　Phone: (502) 426-8950

Web: www.state.ky.us/agencies/parks/tomsawyr.htm

Best known for the following unique amenities: an archery park, a radio controlled airfield, a summer aquatics program, the bicycle motto-cross track or indoor team sports in the park's gymnasium. There's also a few miles of hiking trails.

JEFFERSON MEMORIAL FOREST

11311 Mitchell Hill Road
(I-265 exit 8, southern edge of Jefferson County)

Louisville (Fairdale) 40118

❑　Phone: (502) 368-5404. **Web: www.memorialforest.com**
❑　Hours: Dawn to dusk
❑　Admission: FREE

The forest is a woodland tribute to the area citizens who served in the nation's wars. Dedicated as a National Audubon Wildlife Sanctuary, the land has over 5000 acres of forest with streams, birds and wildlife, steep slopes of second growth woods of pine, oak and chestnut. Recreation areas, nature trails and a welcome center serve as starting points for nature walks and star-gazing programs.

HENRY'S ARK

7801 Rose Island Road (the farm borders the Ohio River - 10 miles from Louisville off US 42)

Louisville (Prospect) 40059

❑   Phone: (502) 228-0746
❑   Hours: Tuesday-Sunday daylight hours (9:00am-sunset)
❑   Admission: FREE. $1.00 donation encouraged.

A privately owned unique petting zoo situated on a 600+ acre horse and cattle farm. Unique because most of its inhabitants are touchable. Tour the outback by trolley and get close-up to larger animals like bison, elk, yak and watusi cattle and smaller animals like ponies, donkeys, sheep and goats. Visitors are encouraged to bring carrots, celery and soda crackers to hand feed the animals. The Ark also furnishes alfalfa cubes for trolley passengers to hand feed bison and elk. The closest you'll ever get to playing "Zookeeper" without extensive training!

KENTUCKY RAILWAY MUSEUM

136 South Main Street (BG Parkway exit 10; SRKY 52 or US 31E between Bardstown & Hodgenville)

New Haven 40051

❑   Phone: (502) 549-5470 or (800) 272-0152
    Web: www.kyrail.org
❑   Hours: Museum: Monday-Saturday 10:00am-4:00pm, Sunday 1:00-4:00pm (March-December). Rail Ride: Weekends (March-May and October-mid December). Tuesday-Sunday (May-September). Departures at Noon or 2:00pm - Boston Depot. Departures at 11:00am or 2:00pm (Saturday) - New Haven Depot.

Kentucky Railway Museum (cont.)

❑   Admission: Museum only: $3.00 adult, $1.00 child (2-12). Train
    ticket (includes museum): $12.50 adult, $8.00 child (2-12).
    Higher fares for Steam Weekends & Locomotive Cab Rides (ride
    with the engineers).

❑   Miscellaneous: Museum Gift Shop with lots of railroad-themed
    items. See seasonal & Special Events chapter for events
    including train robberies and special holiday train rides. Call
    ahead to see if "Thomas the Tank Engine" is visiting this year
    (usually mid-July)!

Ride through a scenic and historic Rolling Fork River Valley. Pass
woodlands, farmlands and small communities. Learn about the
engine and coaches you are riding on. The 22 mile, 1 ½ hour
journey is powered by steam or diesel locomotive carrying
authentic coaches on the rails. The museum houses a collection of
artifacts and memorabilia in a replica of the original New Haven
depot. The kids love the sleeping car exhibit, serving cart, railway
post office and track bicycle inspection car. You can also watch
several different toy train layouts operate in the model train center.
Also see some layouts under construction. The train ride is smooth
- parents could bring a magazine and the kids maybe an activity
book. A Railway Coloring Book (given to each child on the trip
back) is a fun souvenir (be sure to bring your own crayons).

BUFFALO CROSSING

1140 Bagdad Road (I-64 exit 35, take SR 53 north to SR 43 east to
Hwy 12 for 1 mile)

Shelbyville 40065

❑   Phone: (502) 647-0377 or (877) 700-0047
    Web: www.buffalocrossing.com

❑   Hours: Tuesday-Sunday 11:00am-9:00pm.

❑   Tours: Trolley Ride: 45 minute scenic ride to animal exhibit,
    through fields of Buffalo and tour of 1000 acre farm. By
    reservation or special event, small admission fee.

Buffalo Crossing is located on Bluegrass Bison, a 1,000-acre,
working buffalo ranch. Visitors to Buffalo Crossing can catch a

glimpse of live buffalo (look for the largest, Chief Joseph) grazing in their natural habitat, as well as visit a unique petting zoo featuring small frontier animals and large exotic animals alike. Restaurant available.

KENTUCKY SPEEDWAY

(I-71 exit 57 or 55, follow signs)

Sparta 41095

❏   Phone: (888) 652-RACE or (859) 647-4309

Web: www.kentuckyspeedway.com

A 1.5 mile tri-oval, state-of-the-art NASCAR track that opened the summer of 2000. Call or visit website for racing schedule.

LINCOLN HOMESTEAD STATE PARK

5079 Lincoln Park Road (BG Parkway to US 150 east or SRKY 555 south. On SRKY 528 and 438)

Springfield 40069

❏   Phone: (859) 336-7461. **www.kystateparks.com/linchome.htm**
❏   Hours: Park - dawn to dusk. Museum: Daily 8:00am-6:00pm (May-September).
❏   Admission to Museum: $1.00-$2.00 (age 6+).
❏   Miscellaneous: Gift shop, picnicking.

The Berry Home - Nancy Hanks lived in this home when she was courted by Thomas Lincoln. In the huge living room before the immense fireplace, Thomas proposed to Nancy. A copy of their marriage bond hangs there. In the knolls near the Beech Fork River, the buildings are filled with pioneer furniture. The buildings on site are replicas of the 1782 cabin and blacksmith shop where Lincoln's father was reared and learned his trade. It was also the home of Mordecai Lincoln, a favorite uncle of the President.

TAYLORSVILLE LAKE STATE PARK

PO Box 205 (I-64 exit 32, take KY 55 south to KY 44/KY 248 east)

Taylorsville 40071

❑   Phone: (502) 477-8713 or (502) 477-8766 marina

Web: www.state.ky.us/agencies/parks/taylorlk.htm

This park boasts a new campground perfect for the numerous fishermen or equestrians that love the fishing and horse trails through forested countryside. The Visitor's Center (KY 2239) is a pioneer homestead and the Dam Visitor's Center and Overlook has a theatre and trail to the historic homestead. There's also a marina and boat rentals.

MUSIC RANCH USA

407 South Street (off Hwy 31W)

West Point 40177

❑   Phone: (502) 922-9393. **Web: www.musicranch.com**

❑   Hours: Show every Saturday at 7:30pm. Other music shows vary, mostly Friday nights.

❑   Admission: $8.00 adult, $3.00 child (3-11).

❑   Miscellaneous: Chow hall adjacent, open 5:30pm - midnight.

Country jamboree with old time rock, blues, some Bluegrass and gospel.

Chapter 2
Area - North East (NE)

Our Favorites...

* Candy Factories - Lexington Area

* Kentucky Horse Park - Lexington

* Lexington Children's Museum - Lexington

* Kentucky Folk Art Center - Morehead

* Newport Aquarium - Newport

* Carter Caves State Resort Park - Olive Hill

* Daniel Boone National Forest - Winchester

* Big Bone Lick State Park - Union

"Moonwalkers" - Lexington Children's Museum

HIGHLANDS MUSEUM & DISCOVERY CENTER

1620 Winchester Avenue (I-64 to US 23 right into town)

Ashland 41105

❑   Phone: (606) 329-8888. **Web: www.highlandsmuseum.com**

❑   Hours: Tuesday-Saturday 10:00am-4:00pm. Closed New Years, July 4, Thanksgiving and Christmastime.

❑   Admission: $3.00-$3.50 per person (age 2+).

The Country music exhibit features the Judds... but there's lots more to look at in the Children's Discovery Center. Also see displays on Appalachian culture, Native American artifacts, industrial heritage of the area, antique clothing and a "Granny" Toothman spinner/weaver. Interactive areas change twice a year. Look for hands-on exhibits about pioneer exploring, air flight, or life on the river.

COUNTRY MUSIC HIGHWAY 23

(Maps available in downtown Ashland or downtown Paintsville)

Ashland / Paintsville 41105

❑   Phone: (800) 542-5790

US 23 in Kentucky is a tribute to Eastern Kentucky country music stars including The Judds, Tom T. Hall, Billy Ray Cyrus, Ricky Skaggs, and Patty Loveless. In Ashland, stop for a bite at the Country Music Hwy. Café. Butcher Hollow is the birthplace of Loretta Lynn "The Coal Miner's Daughter" and her sister, Crystal Gayle. Located seven miles from downtown Paintsville, souvenirs of Loretta and Crystal are available at the No. 5 General Store owned by their brother Herman Webb. Herman will give you a personal tour of the home (for $5.00 per person), still furnished as it was years ago. Loretta and family memorabilia is scattered throughout. Any country music fan will want to say they visited. SRKY 321 and SRKY 1107 north to SRKY 302 east, then follow signs off Miller's Creek.

DINSMORE HOMESTEAD

5656 Burlington Pike (I-75/71 exit 181 to KY 18 west)

Burlington 41005

❑   Phone: (859) 586-6117. **Web: www.dinsmorefarm.org**
❑   Hours: Wednesday, Saturday, Sunday 1:00-5:00pm (April thru mid-December). Last tour leaves at 4:00pm.
❑   Admission: $5.00 adult, $3.00 senior (60+), $2.00 student (7-17).

A Living History Farm with a museum and nature center on the farm of the Dinsmore family who originally came from the deep south. Learn of their benevolent treatment of slaves. Day Camps, Discovery Days or School Living History (hands-on) Tours are your best bet to take advantage of this facility.

BB RIVERBOATS

Covington Landing Docks or Newport Levee Docks (I-75 Exit 192)

Covington 41011

❑   Phone: (877) BB-is-fun. **Web: www.bbriverboats.com**
❑   Admission: $13.00+ adult, $9.00+ senior, $7.00+ child (4-12). Prices for meal cruises - generally add $10.00+ if entertainment.
❑   Tours: 1-2 hour sightseeing cruises on the Ohio River. Several times daily. Reservations required. May-October.

Docked at the foot of Madison Street, see the modern sternwheelers or old-time steamboat. Also theme cruises like mini-vacation, holiday or historical. Many cruises offer additional lunch, brunch and dinner cruise options. Sightseeing only cruises offer history of the river plus points of interest on the riverfront.

BEHRINGER / CRAWFORD MUSEUM

1600 Montague Road (I-75, exit either 5th Street or 12th Street/Pike Street, follow signs to Devou Park)

Covington 41011

❑   Phone: (859) 491-4003
❑   Hours: Tuesday-Friday 10:00am-5:00pm, Saturday-Sunday 1:00-5:00pm. Closed holidays.
❑   Admission: $3.00

Permanent exhibits include galleries focusing on: Paleontology; Archaeology - detailing prehistoric Native American cultures; Kentucky, Naturally! focusing on local wildlife; 19th Century History featuring home life, politics, Underground Railroad & the Civil War; and River Heritage specializing in steamboats and tugs.

CARNEGIE VISUAL & PERFORMING ARTS CENTER

1028 Scott Blvd.

Covington 41011

❑   Phone: (859) 491-2030. **Web: www.kentuckycenter.org/kapn**

Four art galleries showcase regional artists. Free year-round arts education programs for youth (ArtStop). The theatre hosts a variety of performance events including Christmas and Appalachia productions and workshops on things like making drums.

MAINSTRASSE VILLAGE

616 Main Street (I-75 exit 192)

Covington 41011

❑   Phone: (859) 491-0458 or (800) STAY-NKY
   Web: www.mainstrasse.org
❑   Miscellaneous: Northern Kentucky Visitors Center next to bell tower. Goose Girl bronze sculpture 2 blocks east of tower.

Ongoing restoration and revitalization of a 30 block area in west Covington is now a village with shops and restaurants (try some sweets at the Strudel Shop near the Tower). A favorite with kids is the Carroll Chimes Bell Tower in Goebel Park. The 100 foot bell tower with a 43 bell carillon plays on the hour, from 9:00am-dusk, spring thru Christmas. The bell tower contains one of the 2 American-made animated clocks in the world, with 21 figures performing "The Pied Piper of Hamelin".

RAILWAY EXPOSITION MUSEUM

315 West Southern Avenue

Covington 41011

❑ Phone: (859) 491-7245

❑ Hours: Saturday-Sunday 12:30-4:30pm (May-October)

❑ Admission: $4.00 general

Interiors of railroad cars, railroad memorabilia and locomotives are displayed at this educational museum.

KINCAID LAKE STATE PARK

Rural Route 1, Box 33 (I-275 east to US 27 south to KY 159)

Falmouth 41040

❑ Phone: (859) 654-3531

Web: www.state.ky.us/agencies/parks/kincaid2.htm

A great big campground with a giant lake make this popular for fishermen, boaters and campers. Great for watersports, hiking trails, pedal boats, outdoor pool, tennis and mini-golf too.

GEORGETOWN / SCOTT COUNTY MUSEUM

229 East Main Street (US 25N)

Georgetown 40324

❑ Phone: (502) 863-6201. **Web: www.georgetownky.com**

❑ Hours: Monday-Friday 9:00am-4:00pm

❑ Admission: FREE

The carved oak tree wooden sculpture is probably most talked about at this museum housed in the old Post Office building. The museum also has a video to watch, a timeline and several exhibits.

TOYOTA MOTOR MANUFACTURING KENTUCKY

1001 Cherry Blossom Way (I-75 exit 126 east - US 62 E, follow signs to "Visitor's Entrance"), Georgetown 40324

❑ Phone: (502) 868-3027 or (800) TMM-4485

Web: www.toyotageorgetown.com

For updates visit our website: www.kidslovepublications.com

- Hours: Visitor Center - 9:00am-4:00pm weekdays; to 7:00pm on Thursdays only.
- Admission: FREE
- Public Tours: Monday-Friday, 10:00am, Noon, and 2:00pm; with additional 6:00pm tour on Thursday only. Closed major holidays and 3rd week of July. Reservations strongly encouraged. Those without may tour as space permits. Children must be at least 1st graders and accompanied by an adult. School tours are available for grades 4-12.

Can you imagine a building so BIG that it could house over 156 football fields side by side! Wow! When you arrive and begin your tour of Toyota's state-of-the-art North American manufacturing facility, you and your kids will certainly appreciate that you won't have to walk for this tour. Begin your tour at the Visitor's Center where you get a great taste of what to expect through several interactive exhibits that teach you all about the Toyota JIT (Just in Time) manufacturing philosophy. After viewing a short informational film, you'll board an electric tram (complete with headphones – no loud factory noises here!), to take you on your journey. See steel coils weighing over 34,000 lbs. pressed into body panels and over 700 robots working in precision to create both sedans and mini-vans at this plant. In fact, this is the only manufacturing facility in the world where you will see both vans and cars on the same assembly line at the same time (how do they do that!). Kids will especially love the welding robots that send sparks flying to the factory ceiling (viewed from a safe distance). There are over 4000 welds in each vehicle made. Make sure you tell your kids to watch for the "flying assembly workers" who float in and out of vehicles on specially made chairs (on long booms). The Toyota tire "Yo-Yo" available at the gift shop is a great way to remember this visit!

CINCINNATI BENGALS SUMMER TRAINING CAMP

400 East College Street (I-75 and I-64, just 10 miles north of Lexington at the Georgetown College Athletic Complex)

Georgetown 40324

- ❑ Phone: (502) 868-6588. **Web: www.bengalscamp.com**
- ❑ Hours: Mid-July thru Mid-August.
- ❑ Admission: FREE, fee for parking (usually around $10.00 per vehicle).

Bengals fans can see what the coaches see as the team is forming for the upcoming season of football. FanFest, with activities such as NFL inflatable obstacle course is run during this pre-season camp.

GREENBO LAKE STATE RESORT PARK

HC 60 Box 562 (I-64 Grayson exit on KY 1 north)

Greenup 41144

- ❑ Phone: (606) 473-7324 or (800) 325-0083
  Web: www.state.ky.us/agencies/parks/greenbo2.htm

The name Jesse Stuart (author, educator, Kentucky Poet Laureate and a native of Greenup County) is found throughout these hills at both the lodge and state nature preserve. Read the poet's work in the reading room, swim in the lakeside pool with waterslide, children's wading pool and mist fountains or hike in secluded forests and trails (the Jenny Wiley Trail Heritage Byway). There's also a campground, marina and rental boats, pool, tennis and mini-golf.

UK BASKETBALL MUSEUM

410 Vine Street (Civic Center Shops, 2nd Floor)

Lexington 40501

- ❑ Phone: (859) 225-5670 or (800) 269-1953
  Web: www.ukbballmuseum.org
- ❑ Hours: Monday-Saturday 10:00am-5:00pm, Sunday Noon-5:00pm.
- ❑ Admission: $5.00 adult, $3.00 student.

For updates visit our website: www.kidslovepublications.com

Here they highlight the history of the Nation's most outstanding college basketball programs with lots of video footage of Wildcat play displayed with premium memorabilia. As you walk through the museum, don't just look - experience: Call play-by-play for one of your favorite Wildcat games, test your knowledge at a trivia station, experience mind-blowing audio/visual exhibits, compare UK history with World events, or learn about the sciences of basketball and nutrition. Be sure to look for the ultimate "virtual court" which pits you against some of Kentucky's greatest players or take your picture next to your favorite player's action statue.

ASHLAND, THE HENRY CLAY ESTATE

120 Sycamore Road (I-75 exit 104, turn left, go 7.5 miles. Corner of Sycamore and US 25/KY 922)

Lexington 40502

❑   Phone: (859) 266-8581. **Web: www.henryclay.org**
❑   Hours: Monday-Saturday 10:00am-4:00pm, Sunday 1:00-
        4:00pm.Closed Mondays (November-March). Closed January
        and holidays.
❑   Admission: $7.00 adult, $3.00 child (6-12).
❑   Tours: one hour long - guided, given on the hour.
❑   Miscellaneous: Food is available in the Café open for lunch and
        snacks. Museum Store.

Henry Clay (1777-1852) was named The Great Compromiser, Harry of the West, Candidate for President and quoted "I'd rather be right than president". Living here most of his adult life, the 18 room mansion is furnished with Clay family possessions. The tour begins with a videotape historical review. On tour, there are also outbuildings on the grounds like the icehouse, smokehouse, dairy cellar, privy/laundry and keepers cottage - all in a park-like setting.

OLD KENTUCKY CANDIES

450 Southland Drive (I-75 exit 115 west to Harrodsburg Rd, right on
Lane Allen Road to Southland)

Lexington 40503

❑   Phone: (859) 278-4444 or (800) 786-0579
     Web: www.oldkycandy.com
❑   Admission: FREE
❑   Tours: Monday-Thursday 10:00am-12:30pm and 1:30-3:00pm.
     45 minutes. Best to call ahead for production hours. 8 to 50
     people for tours. Reservations please.

Hopefully you'll go on a day when you can watch them make
Kentucky Derby Mints or UK molded chocolates. Plenty of samples
follow the tour that includes verbal and photo explanations.

MC CONNELL SPRINGS

416 Rebmann Lane
(New Circle to Old Frankfort Pike, exit 6 south, follow signs)

Lexington 40504

❑   Phone: (859) 225-4073
     www.lfucg.com/parksrec/mcconnellsprings.asp
❑   Hours: Daily 9:00am-5:00pm.

The campsite of the first settlers in the Bluegrass. McConnell
Springs is the site where Lexington was founded. It lies within a
tract of land claimed by William McConnell in 1775. McConnell
Springs has over two miles of trails that wander past historic
foundations, stone fences, an old farm pond and lush vegetation.
The new Education Center is equipped with a lab with sinks and
counter space allowing students to conduct hands-on experiments
and textbook research.

PARKETTE DRIVE-IN

1216 E. New Circle Road (between Winchester Road and
Richmond road)

Lexington 40505

❑   Phone: (859) 254-8723

❑ Hours: Monday-Thursday 10:00am-10:30pm; Friday & Saturday 10:00am-11:30pm; Sunday 11:00am-9:00pm.

Very economically priced (combo meals are under $4.00), this place is a step back in time. Since 1951, this "drive-in" ordering eatery is right out of scenes of "Happy Days". After placing your order over the microphone, a delivery girl or boy (adorned in Parkette cap and t-shirt remeninscent of the 50's) delivers your order window-side. Their menu includes burgers, fried chicken, seafood and the famous "Kentucky Poor Boy" sandwich (double-decker burgers dressed with toppings to the hilt!). Memories meet the pavement when (on Friday nights) the Parkette is host to classic cars and motorcycles. They serve 12,000 customers a week.

UNIVERSITY OF KENTUCKY

South Limestone Street (Visitor Center is at UK Student Center - off Avenue of Champions -Bounded by Limestone Street, Euclid Ave., and Rose Street)

Lexington 40506

❑ Phone: (859) 257-9000

   Web: www.uky.edu (campus guide/map)

❑ Admission: FREE

❑ Tours: Walking tours are conducted Monday-Friday at 10:00am and 2:00pm (also Saturday at 11:00am during the academic year). Guided tours of the campus depart from the visitors center in the Student Center on Euclid Avenue across from Memorial Coliseum.

The 625 acre campus was established in 1865 and enrolls 24,000 students.

UK ART MUSEUM - Singletary Center for the Arts at the corner of Euclid and Rose Streets. Changing shows of permanent and traveling exhibits. Tours available. Tuesday-Sunday, Noon-5:00pm. Closed July 4, Thanksgiving, and Christmas thru New Years. (859) 257-5716.

University of Kentucky (cont.)

WEBB MUSEUM OF ANTHROPOLOGY - Lafferty Hall, center of campus. Traces history of humans in Kentucky. Other displays highlight the artistry, ingenuity and technology of present-day cultures from around the world. Monday-Friday 8:00am-4:30pm. Closed holidays. (859) 257-7112.

COLDSTREAM & MAINE CHANCE FARMS - Newtown Park. Used by UK for crop and livestock research. North of downtown near I-64/75.

ARBORETUM PARK - "A Walk Across Kentucky" showcases state vegetation grouped by region. Open dawn to dusk. Children's Garden - Alphabet plants and plantings in old tennis shoes. Master Gardener - demo Veggie Garden, Fish Pond, plants for Kentucky gardens. Be sure to get a colorful map and have fun playing the Arboretum Garden Game. (859) 257-9339.

CENTRAL KENTUCKY YOUTH ORCHESTRA

161 North Mill Street (ArtsPlace office)

Lexington 40507

❑   Phone: (859) 254-0796. **Web: www.ckyo.org**

Two orchestras and over 140 talented young people perform children's concerts. Performed at the Singletary Center or the Opera House, September through May.

LEXINGTON CHILDREN'S THEATRE

418 West Short Street (downtown)

Lexington 40507

❑   Phone: (859) 254-9565. **Web: www.lctonstage.org**
❑   Admission: $12.00 each or subscription discount Flex-Tix pricing.

Charlotte's Web, a Christmas Carol, and A Wind in the Willows are examples of the many folklore-based plays offered. Plays are rated for age appropriateness (ex. Age 4+ or Age 9+).

LEXINGTON LEGENDS BASEBALL

Applebee's Park, 1200 North Broadway,

Lexington 40507

❑   Phone: (859) 422-7867. Web: www.lexingtonlegends.com

They may be a Single A team, but Lexington has quickly embraced their new team in a major league way and the seats are packed for home games. The park has a family picnic area and kids play area. The season runs from April to September. Tickets run $3.00-$7.00.

LEXINGTON PHILHARMONIC

161 North Mill Street (ArtsPlace), **Lexington** 40507

❑   Phone: (859) 233-7896 or (859) 233-4226 tickets
    Web: www.lexingtonphilharmonic.org

The Family Series (one-hour musical and visual with activities) and Pops Concerts (Patriotic Concert, Kentucky Christmas Chorus, two free concerts and Picnic with the Pops).

LEXINGTON BALLET

161 North Mill Street (ArtsPlace office), **Lexington** 40507

❑   Phone: (859) 233-3925. Web: www.lexingtonballet.org

Dance training and arts education programs. With several classic, children's and romantic ballet performances like the Nutcracker & Swan Lake.

LEXINGTON CHILDREN'S MUSEUM

440 West Main Street (Victorian Square, corner of W. Short and Algonquin Streets),

Lexington 40507

❑   Phone: (859) 258-3256
    Web: www.lexingtonchildrensmuseum.com
❑   Hours: Tuesday-Saturday 10:00am-5:00pm, Sunday 1:00-
    5:00pm. Closed Mondays rest of year. Closed Easter, week after
    Labor Day, Thanksgiving and Christmas.
❑   Admission: $4.00 per person (age 1+). Free parking for up to 3
    hours in Victorian Square Garage.

Lexington Children's Museum (cont.)

❑ Miscellaneous: While you're downtown, stop by Thoroughbred Park on Main Street where 7 life size bronze statues of horses racing are available to climb on for great photo ops!

Hands-on exhibits cover science, nature, history, civics and ecology. Little ones can visit the Toddler Sensory Area (under age 3 - hear, touch and see nesting areas). Everyone will love to make huge bubbles in the Bubble Factory; go Home to world geography and culture; "Walk on the Moon" and even sit in a crater!; create Soil Wars; make a Quake; be a Turtle; Greet the Brainzilla (giant brain that talks to you); Walk thru a Human Heart with many "chamber" rooms; make Me and My Shadow; or play a King Piano. Extremely well done exhibits include descriptions that are easy to follow and teach to the children. Those living in the area should become members so they can attend the interesting monthly workshops. Exhibits change each season, so there is something new to explore. Look for occasional new Dinofriends, the Bubble car, or the Kids Zone. While you're in the Victorian Square area, stop over for soup and sandwich topped off with an old-fashioned soda dessert at Hutchinson's Drug Store. Have fun!

HUNT-MORGAN HOUSE

201 North Mill Street (near 2nd Street, downtown)

Lexington 40508

❑ Phone: (859) 253-0362 or 233-3290
Web: www.bluegrasstrust.org/hunt-morgan/index.htm
❑ Admission: $7.00 adult, $4.00 student with ID.
❑ Tours: Guided tours Tuesday-Saturday 10:00am-4:00pm, Sunday 2:00-5:00pm (mid-March to mid-December). Closed Thanksgiving. Tours begin ¼ past the hour.

An 1800's Federal-style prominent family home of the Hunt-Morgan families. John Wesley Hunt was the first millionaire of the west (and built this home). John Hunt Morgan was the "Thunderbolt of the Confederacy" and Thomas Hunt Morgan was the "father of modern genetics" and a Nobel Prize winner. The architecture of a fan-light doorway and cantilevered staircase mixed with original furnishings and Civil War memorabilia, make this a piece of history based on its inhabitants.

MARY TODD LINCOLN HOUSE

578 West Main Street (just a block down from the Rupp Arena)

Lexington 40508

❑ Phone: (859) 233-9999. **Web: www.mtlhouse.org**
❑ Hours: Monday-Saturday 10:00am-4:00pm (March 15-November). Closed holidays.
❑ Admission: $7.00 adult, $4.00 child (6-12)
❑ Tours: Last tour begins 45 minutes before closing. Guided, one hour.

The girlhood home of Abraham Lincoln's wife, Mary. The two story, beautiful brick 1803 Georgian-style house is furnished with period furniture from Mary's collection and personal articles of the Lincoln-Todd families. Kids like hearing stories about a famous adult's life as a child. Did you know that Mary had 15 brothers and sisters and that she had a formal education of 12 years (vs. her husband who really had very little)? Opposites attract.

KENTUCKY HORSE PARK

4089 Iron Works Parkway (I-75 exit 120)

Lexington 40511

❑ Phone: (859) 233-4303 or (800) 678-8813
Web: www.kyhorsepark.com
❑ Hours: Daily 9:00am-5:00pm (March 15-October). Closed on Mondays and Tuesdays (November-March 14). Closed Thanksgiving, Christmas, and New Years.
❑ Admission: $10.00+ adult, Approximately half price for child (7-12). Additional special exhibit fees are added on during peak season (late spring thru late summer). Children 6 and under free when accompanied by paying adult. Reduced tickets available for the Winter Season (approximately half price but less activities available).

Kentucky Horse Park (cont.)

❑   Miscellaneous: Clubhouse Restaurant, Campgrounds, Gift Shop, Horseback rides ($13+), Pony rides ($13+), Nearly 60 horse shows are held here yearly. Visits with Mares and Foals daily presentation in June/July.

Do you have a real horse lover in the family? This is a horse-lover's dream park. It's Kentucky's tribute to one of its famous industries from tiny minis to large draft horses to retired racing stars. Begin with the Visitor Info Center Film - wide screen film "Thou Shalt Fly Without Wings" - depicting man's special relationship with horses both at work and play. Now, go next door to the International Museum of the Horse. Before long, take the horse-drawn trolley tour.   Then catch a show at the Hall of Champions - home of retired "equine millionaires" (3x daily). They tell you funny stories about famous horses. Also be sure to catch a show at the Parade of Breeds - show of dozens of breeds of horses with their riders in native costume with music accompaniment (2x daily). Some are used for rugged terrain, pulling, cowboy riding, cavalry, or trailing. Fill the time between shows at the Big Barn (talk with trainers), Draft and Breeds and Carriage Barns, farrier's and harness maker's shops.   The American Saddle Horse Museum - is a multi-image show and exhibit hall located on the premises near the parking lots. (800-829-4438).

WAVELAND STATE HISTORIC SITE

225 Waveland Museum Lane, 225 Higbee Mill Road (Off US 27, south of downtown)

Lexington 40514

❑   Phone: (859) 272-3611
      Web: www.kystateparks.com/agencies/parks/wavelan2.htm
❑   Hours: Monday-Saturday 10:00am-5:00pm, Sunday 1:00-5:00pm (April - mid-December).
❑   Admission: $6.00 adult, $5.00 senior, $3.00 student (age 6+).
❑   Tours: On the hour, last tour 4:00pm. Tours last approximately 1.5 hours.

❑   Miscellaneous: Picnicking. Country Picnic and tours (meal and tour
        several days each week in June, small additional fee for food).

This beautiful 1847 Greek Revival home was built by Joseph
Bryan, a grand-nephew of Daniel Boone. Tours focus on the
everyday lives of the Bryan Family and the African-Americans
who lived and worked there. Waveland exemplifies plantation life
in Kentucky in the 19th-century; from the acres of grain and hemp
waving in the breeze (hence the Waveland name), to the raising
and racing of blooded trotting horses. Included are the icehouse,
smokehouse and servants quarters.

RAVEN RUN NATURE SANCTUARY

5888 Jacks Creek Road (off US 25/421 south)

Lexington 40515

❑   Phone: (859) 272-6105
❑   Hours: Daily 9:00am-7:00pm (April-September). 9:00am-
        5:00pm, rest of year. Trails close 30 minutes before park closing.
        Closed Thanksgiving and Christmas.
❑   Admission: FREE

Follow trails lined with native flora and fauna, rock fences, a
historic home, meadow, forest and creeks leading to views of the
Kentucky River palisades. The park is also known for the
waterfalls and wildflowers. Stop at the nature center too.

AVIATION MUSEUM OF KENTUCKY

**4000 Versailles Road (2 miles west of New Circle Rd. on US 60 to
Bluegrass Airport Road)**

Lexington 40544

❑   Phone: (859) 231-1219. **Web: www.aviationky.org**
❑   Hours: Tuesday-Saturday 10:00-5:00pm, Sunday 1:00-5:00pm.
        Closed Thanksgiving, Christmas and New Years.
❑   Admission: $2.00-$4.00 (age 6+).

Most interesting to kids is the cockpit you can sit in, the supersonic
trainer, and the "Women in Aviation" display. There's also lots of
uniforms, model airplanes, actual aircraft (helicopters, a Skyhawk
II, and a Quadraplane).

KEENELAND TRACK KITCHEN

4201 Versailles Road (US 60 west)

Lexington 40592

- ❏ Phone: (859) 253-0541. **Web: www.keeneland.com**
- ❏ Hours: "Breakfast with the Works" buffet served during morning workouts during seasonal race months (usually April and October) daily 6:00am-10:30am. May be Closed Monday, Tuesday and Easter.
- ❏ Admission: Reasonably priced buffet.

Meet and greet and eat with trainers and jockeys at breakfast during morning workouts.

YATESVILLE LAKE STATE PARK

PO Box 767 (US 23 to Louisa, then west on KY 3)

Louisa 41230

- ❏ Phone: (606) 673-1490 or (606) 686-2361 marina. **Web: www.state.ky.us/agencies/parks/yatesvil.htm**
- ❏ Miscellaneous: Eagle Watch Weekend - houseboat tours on the Lake to the eagle's nesting site. Programs, games and refreshments included in admission.

Full service campsites and marina with rentals are the highlights of this park. The lake and river make for good fishing and along these waters are great scenic overlooks and play areas. The campground has modern and primitive sites. The Mary Ingles Trail is 3 ½ miles of hiking.

MAYSVILLE FLOODWALL MURALS

216 Bridge Street (downtown riverfront)

Maysville 41056

- ❏ Phone: (606) 564-9411
- ❏ Hours: 24 hours a day
- ❏ Admission: FREE

Historical portrayals of the Ohio River by artist Robert Dafford of scouts, nobility who floated down the river, and settlers.

NATIONAL UNDERGROUND RAILROAD MUSEUM

115 East Third Street

Maysville 41056

❑   Phone: (606) 564-6986

     Web: www.coax.net/people/lwf/urmuseum.htm

❑   Hours: Monday-Saturday 10:00am-4:00pm

❑   Admission: Donations

The museum symbolizes a local effort to preserve and display artifacts that tell the stories of life on the Underground Railroad. The Maysville area is surrounded by freedom stations - crossing the Ohio River north was a preeminent step in escaping bondage.

KENTUCKY FOLK ART CENTER

102 West First Street (I-64 exit 137, follow signs)

Morehead 40351

❑   Phone: (606) 783-2204. **Web: www.kyfolkart.org**

❑   Hours: Monday-Saturday 9:00am-5:00pm (yearlong). Sunday
     1:00-5:00pm (April-December).

❑   Admission: $3.00 (12 and over). $2.00 senior. FREE on
     Sundays.

❑   Miscellaneous: Museum Store with original artworks, Library
     and rotating upstairs Gallery.

Visit the only museum of Kentucky Folk Art, housed in a renovated early 1900 grocery warehouse. In the Auditorium, watch a seven minute video narrated by Rosemary Clooney introducing visitors to the "World of Wonder" housed within the Center. Look for recycled material sculpted into George Washington, Dolly Parton, Uncle Sam and Ronald McDonald. There was a birdhouse in an old shoe (that's art?). Our favorite was "Precious Memories" - a monkey made with junk - can you find the cow and chess piece? From whimsical to religious to political statements are made through this art.

MINOR CLARK STATE FISH HATCHERY

120 Fish Hatchery Road (SR 801south (Off I-64), below dam.
Farmers/Sharkey exit)

Morehead 40351

❏ Phone: (606) 784-6872
❏ Hours: Monday-Friday 7:00am-3:00pm. Closed holidays.
   Viewing of display pool and ponds anytime.
❏ Admission: FREE

This is among the largest warm water hatcheries in the country with 300 acres, 111 ponds, and a few racers (give fish a chance to exercise). The display pool is wonderful with large and small largemouth bass, walleye, 2 varieties of striped bass, and muskie to view up close. Their main objective is to produce fish for Kentucky waters to enhance opportunities to catch trophy fish.

MOREHEAD STATE UNIVERSITY

University Blvd.

Morehead 40351

❏ Phone: (606) 784-5221 or (800) 654-1944
   Web: www.morehead-st.edu or www.msueagles.com

Established in 1887, the 500 acre campus enrolls 8300 students and has a history of focusing on Appalachian peoples. The Cora Wilson Stewart Moonlight School building was once used for nighttime reading and writing classes for Appalachian people and an Appalachian Collection is found on the 5th floor of the Camden-Carroll Library Tower. Nearby (KY 377) is the MSU Farm Complex & Arena.

BLUE LICKS BATTLEFIELD STATE RESORT PARK

PO Box 66 (US 68 northeast of Lexington)

Mount Olivet 41064

❏ Phone: (659) 289-5507 or (800) 443-7008
   Web: www.state.ky.us/agencies/parks/bluelick.htm

❑   Hours: Museum: Sunday-Thursday 9:00am-5:00pm, Friday-
      Saturday 9:00am-6:00pm (April-October); Thursday through
      Sunday 9:00am-5:00pm (November-March).

In 1782, Blue Licks was the site of the last Revolutionary War battle in Kentucky. Visit the Pioneer Museum (admission $1.50-$2.00) where you can learn more about the battle plus history of why prehistoric animals, Indians, pioneers and 19th century Southerners came for the salt licks and soothing waters (view a 10 minute video plus tons of relics). The Nature Preserve protects a rare plant - Short's Goldenrod - the only place it's found in the world growing along the rocky buffalo trace. On campus, there's a modern lodge with dining room, cottages, campgrounds, pool, hiking trail, mini-golf and recreation programs.

RUTH HUNT CANDIES

550 North Maysville

Mt. Sterling 40353

❑   Phone: (859) 498-0676 or (800) 927-0302
      Web: www.ruthhuntcandy.com
❑   Admission: FREE
❑   Tours: Monday-Thursday 10:30am-Noon and 1:00-2:30pm. Best
      to make appointment in the summer (less production).
      Reservations for group tours, please

"You are about to taste a little bit of Kentucky's confectionery history!" In the early 1920s, Ruth Hunt made and served homemade sweets to her bridge club. They were so loved that she decided to open a small candy store in her home, packaging products in coffee tins. On tour, you'll see hot cinnamon suckers being formed on a huge old marble slab, giant copper kettles (how old might they be?), and nuts roasting in the oven. Most of these confections are still made from Ruth's original recipes. Their most famous product is the Blue Monday Sweet Bar - the chocolate covered, pulled cream candy center, melt-in-your-mouth legend. Let their Blue Monday sweets cure your "Blue Monday". They are also noted as the official assorted candies of Churchill Downs. The treat at the end is to sample a few fresh sweets!

NEWPORT AQUARIUM

One Aquarium Way (Newport on the Levee, I-71south or I-275 east
to I-471 south exit 5 (Rt. 8) to parking garage).

Newport 41011

- ❑ Phone: (888) 491-FINS. **Web: www.newportaquarium.com**
- ❑ Hours: Daily 10:00am-7:00pm (Summers), Daily 10:00am-
  6:00pm (Fall/Winter/Spring).
- ❑ Admission: $16.00 adult, $14.00 senior (65+), $10.00 child (3-12).
- ❑ Miscellaneous: Lighthouse Café, Gift shop. No strollers past the
  entrance.

As you take the escalator down into the ocean, you'll read thru a
brochure that invites you to explore one million gallons of water.
They use clear, seamless acrylic walls and tunnels that truly make
you want to reach out and touch the fish. Everywhere you go,
remember to look up, look down and keep your ears open - it truly
is a place you have to go using all of your senses. 60 different
exhibits take you places you'd probably never go! Rivers of the
World (knifefish); The Bizarre and Beautiful (flashlight fish);
Pirate Theatre (a movie ship - Yo, Ho, Ho!); Shore Gallery (touch
pool where visitors can feel & examine creatures like Mermaid's
Purses or tickle a Horseshoe Crab); and, Kingdom of Penguins - 16
King Penguins from Japan are set in a winter setting theatre with
video monitor close-ups. Occasionally baby penguins are hatched
and grown in the nursery here! The absolute highlight is the
Surrounded by Sharks exhibit - 85 feet under water! The tunnels
take you thru a shark home - as your child presses his nose against
the acrylic tube - wait - for the first shriek when a shark is sighted
and comes right at you! Don't worry, it's a total thrill that's
completely safe.

WORLD PEACE BELL EXHIBIT CENTER

425 York Street, **Newport** 41011

- ❑ Phone: (859) 261-2526

The World Peace Bell is the world's largest free swinging bell. It
weighs 66,000 lbs., is 12 feet in diameter and 12 feet high. Its
clapper alone weighs an amazing 6,878 pounds. The yoke in which

it swings weighs an additional 16,512 pounds. This magnificent bell rings with a powerful, awe-inspiring, deep resonant tone that is truly a majestic symbol of freedom and peace. Bell swings and rings each day at noon.

CAMP NELSON HERITAGE PARK

6614 Danville Road (US 27 south of Lexington)

Nicholasville 40356

❑   Phone: (859) 881-5716 or (859) 492-3115
     Web: www.campnelson.org
❑   Hours: Tuesday-Saturday 10:00am-5:00pm. Interpretive trails
     open dawn to dusk.

The origin of Camp Nelson is closely linked with President Lincoln's desire to free pro-Union sections of east Tennessee from Confederate control. The camp supplied Union efforts in east Tennessee, central and eastern Kentucky and southwestern Virginia. The only remaining building of the 300 within the camp is the White House which was seized from the residents, the Oliver Perry family. This house served as the Officers' Quarters and is open to tour to depict both the life of the Perry's and military life. A visitor can walk along the interpretive trail and imagine what it would have been like to have been stationed at Camp Nelson.

HARRY MILLER LOCK COLLECTION

1014 South Main Street (Lockmasters Inc. training center)

Nicholasville 40356

❑   Phone: (859) 887-9633
❑   Hours: Monday, Wednesday and Friday from 1:00-4:00pm.
❑   Admission: FREE

See the world's largest lock collection. A brochure details the history of the items showcased. No formal tours available. Self-guided tours only.

CARTER CAVES STATE RESORT PARK

344 Caveland Drive (I-64 west to KY 182 north)

Olive Hill 41164

❑   Phone: (606) 286-4411 or (800) 325-0059

Web: www.state.ky.us/agencies/parks/cartcave.htm

Tour through more than 20 twisting caverns departing from the Welcome Center several times daily ($3.00-5.00). Bat Cave (May-August only) is the protected home of the Social Bat/Indiana Bat. Cascade Cave, with a 30 foot underground waterfall or X Cave with formed luminous stone fans, pipes and spirals are special spots here too. Canoeing down Tygart's Creek (June-August) can be fun or take a guided horseback trail ride. The 20 miles of hiking trails feature such attractions as Box Canyon, Wind Tunnel and Natural Bridge. Property next to this park is Tygart's State Forest with many other trails. Other amenities are a lodge, cottages, campgrounds, a marina with boat rentals, tennis and mini-golf.

GRAYSON LAKE STATE PARK/ SOMEDAY DRAMA

314 Grayson Lake Park Road (I-64 west to exit 172, KY 7 south)

Olive Hill 41164

❑   Phone: (606) 474-9727

Web: www.state.ky.us/agencies/parks/graysonl.htm

Once a favorite campground for Shawnee and Cherokee Indians, this land is full of sheer sandstone canyons and gentle slopes. Camping is still the favorite here, plus a beach/swimming, a boat launch, and hiking trails. Grayson Lake State Park is also the stage for the musical summer drama, "Someday." Set in eastern Kentucky during the Civil War, Someday is the story of a young Confederate captain's efforts to organize a band of partisan rangers, and his love affair with a local girl, whose father is staunchly Union and opposed to his daughter's relationship with the rebel officer. The season starts in June and goes through July, Friday and Saturday performances (tickets: $6.00-$10.00).

For updates visit our website: www.kidslovepublications.com

HOPEWELL MUSEUM

800 Pleasant Street

Paris 40361

❑ Phone: (859) 987-7274

❑ Hours: Wednesday-Saturday, Noon-5:00pm, Sunday 2:00-
4:00pm. (Closed January)

❑ Admission: FREE

Housed in the historic 1909 Beaux Arts-style Paris post office.
The museum features changing exhibits on the art and history of
Bourbon County and central Kentucky. A large exhibit focuses on
Garrett Morgan, an African-American man born in Paris who
invented the tri-color traffic light and gas mask.

BIG BONE LICK STATE PARK

3380 Beaver Road (I-75 AND KY 338, exit 175, follow signs)

Union 41091

❑ Phone: (859) 384-3522

Web: www.state.ky.us/agencies/parks/bigbone.htm

❑ Hours: Museum daily 8:00am-8:00pm (April-October).
Thursday-Monday Noon-5:00pm (November-March). Closed in
January and the week of Christmas.

❑ Admission: Approximately $1.00 per person.

❑ Miscellaneous: Campground, Gift shop, Pool, 2.5 miles of Hiking
Trails, Tennis, Mini Golf, Picnicking.

The birthplace of American Vertebrate Paleontology. The greatest
ice age graveyard ever found! A premier archeological site because
great herds of giant mastodons, mammoths, and bison came to the
warm salt springs (the springs still bubble today). Some became
trapped in the marshy ground and died here, leaving skeletons that
have been uncovered from prehistoric times. A walking diorama,
the outdoor museum hosts these beasts displayed in their natural
habitat. Erosion may still reveal bones (look for them on your hike)
especially along the creek. A live buffalo herd now roams the
property and your kids can touch Mastodon teeth!

BLUEGRASS SCENIC RAILROAD AND MUSEUM

Woodford County Park (US 62 west)

Versailles 40383

❏ Phone: (859) 873-2476 or (800) 755-2476. **Web: www.bgrm.org**
❏ Hours: Museum open every weekend 1:30-3:30pm. (early May thru mid-November).
❏ Admission: $8.00 adult, $7.00 senior (62+), $6.00 child (2-12). Museum free.
❏ Tours: Departures 2-3 times per afternoon. Several Train Robberies and Holiday train weekends too.

Ride on the old Louisville Southern Mainline past horse farms, Kentucky wildflowers, through the rolling Bluegrass Regions, past a 240-foot deep gorge and on to the rugged terrain of the Kentucky River bluffs. The excursions are 1.5 hours long and are narrated. The depot museum is dedicated to the construction, restoration and preservation of the railroad arts and artifacts. Their theme train rides are the best way for younger children to enjoy the long ride (esp. the Clown Days) unless you ride during naptime!

JOUETT HOUSE

255 Craig Creek Road (Off McGowan's Ferry Road west, KY 1064)

Versailles 40383

❏ Phone: (859) 873-7902. **Web: www.jackjouetthouse.org**
❏ Hours: Wednesday 11:00am-4:00pm, Saturday-Sunday 1:00-5:00pm (April-October)
❏ Admission: FREE

Have you ever heard of the "Paul Revere of the South"? Well, by touring the 1798 home of Captain Jack Jouett, you'll learn how he reportedly rode horseback for 40 miles to Charlottesville, VA to warn delegates of the British Invasion. The house contains three rooms with painted fireplace mantels, a stone-lined cellar, and two bedrooms accessed by a sharply turning stairway. Jouett's son, Matthew's famous paintings are also on display.

NOSTALGIA STATION TOY AND TRAIN MUSEUM

279 Depot Street (off US 60 bypass)

Versailles 40383

❑ Phone: (859) 873-2497

❑ Hours: Wednesday-Saturday 10:00am-5:00pm, Sunday 1:00-5:00pm; closed major holidays.

❑ Admission: $1.50-$3.50 (age 3+).

A model train museum housed in a restored 1911 railroad station with exhibits of a reproduction of a 1926 Lionel train display and many children's toys. The displays are meticulously authentic to the original time period.

HARRIET BEECHER STOWE SLAVERY TO FREEDOM MUSEUM

2124 Main Street

Washington 41096

❑ Phone: (606) 759-0505

❑ Hours: Saturday Noon-4:00pm, Sunday 1:00-4:00pm.

❑ Admission: Donations accepted.

This is where the author of "Uncle Tom's Cabin" first witnessed a slave auction (1833) described in the book. The facility shows facets of a slaves life including shackles and art.

DANIEL BOONE NATIONAL FOREST

1700 Bypass Road (KY 801), **Winchester** 40391

❑ Phone: (859) 745-3100

Web: www.southernregion.fs.fed.us/boone

❑ Hours: 24 hours a day. Specific hours for facilities within the park are listed below.

❑ Admission: FREE

The U.S. Forest Service maintains almost 700,000 acres of timberland in portions of 21 counties in eastern Kentucky stretching from Morehead in the north to the Tennessee border in the southeast. 800 miles of paved road and 500 miles of trails make the natural beauty and recreational facilities accessible (campgrounds, picnic and shelter areas, beaches and boat ramps - most on KY 801). Some facilities featured:

GIANT CANADA GEESE OBSERVATION AREA - largest of 11 subspecies of Canada geese. Mature ganders may have a wind span of 6 feet. Observation deck and interpretive trail.

CAVE RUN LAKE - I-64 exit 133, south on KY 801. 8000+ acre lake with 13 ramps, two marinas, 3 campgrounds, boating, swimming, horseback riding, mountain biking and hiking trails and fishing. Cave Run Dam is on KY 826 off KY 801 and has recreation facilities. The Cave Run Lake Morehead Ranger Visitor Center is two miles south of US 60 and has exhibits and a video presentation about the lake area. (606) 784-5624 from 8:00am-4:30pm (Memorial day thru October) and open weekdays only the rest of the year.

PIONEER WEAPONS HUNTING AREA - US 60, south on KY 211 at Salt Lick to Rd. 129. Over 7000 acres full of hiking and primitive weapons (only!) hunting of deer, turkey, grouse, squirrel, fox and raccoon. (606) 784-6428.

SHELTOWEE TRACE NATIONAL RECREATION TRAIL - almost 300 miles of trails. Sheltowee means " Big Turtle" and was the Indian name given Daniel Boone by the Shawnee who adopted him as the son of Blackfish, the great Indian war chief.

RED RIVER GORGE - Mountain Pkwy. Exit 33 at Slade is 27,000 acres of spectacular boulder-strewn areas of woodland, streams and waterfalls, sandstone cliffs, overlooks, arches, the Nada old logging railroad tunnel, and rare plant and animal life. The Visitor Info Station is the Gladie Historic Site (606) 663-2825, on KY 715, and has info on recreation in the Forest. Open daily 10:00am-6:00pm (April-October). The Gladie Historic Site is a restored log cabin (c. 1880) with displays of early logging and farm life and many seasonal events. Here you'll find more information on the 38 miles of 150 sandstone arches - Gray's Arch on KY 15E being a stop where you can picnic on the ridge. Clifty Wilderness off KY 15W are vertical sandstone cliffs, numerous arches, rock houses (cliff overhangs used as shelter by primitive peoples), rippling streams, waterfalls, primitive camping, hiking and canoeing. Rock Bridge off KY 15W is a stone arch spanning Swift Camp Creek and Sky Bridge is another stone arch at the top of the ridge with a vista of the Red River Gorge.

BEAVER CREEK PUBLIC WILDLIFE AREA - off US 27S in the west, KY 90 & Rd. 817 to the east. Hiking, trout fishing, primitive camping and horseshoes.

NATURAL ARCH SCENIC AREA - off US 27S. Sandstone arch that's 100 feet wide and 60 feet high. (606) 679-2010.

71

Chapter 3
Area - South Central (SC)

Our Favorites...

* Corvette Assembly Plant - Bowling Green

* Lost River Cave & Valley - Bowling Green

* Mammoth Cave Area, Amusement, Museums - Cave City

* Wigwam Village - Cave City

* McDowell House & Apothecary - Danville

* Kentucky Down Under - Horse Cave

* Big South Fork Area - Stearns

* Lake Cumberland Area

"Corvette Fun" - Bowling Green

NOLIN LAKE STATE PARK

PO Box 340 (Follow the Western Kentucky Parkway to Leitchfield exit (107) onto KY 259 South. Then, access from KY 728 and KY 1827 north), **Bee Springs** 42207

❑   Phone: (270) 286-4240

   Web: www.state.ky.us/agencies/parks/nolnlake.htm

The 5500+ acre lake is popular for boating and fishing with a marina and beach near the park. Facilities include boat rentals, cottages, camping and picnic areas.

BEECH BEND PARK

798 Beech Bend Road (31W south to Riverview Ave turns into Beech Bend Rd, I-65 exit 28)

Bowling Green 42101

❑   Phone: (270) 781-7634. **Web: www.beechbend.com**

❑   Hours: Daily (Memorial Day-Labor Day) and weekends only (May, September) for Amusement Park. Car racing is offered March - November, usually Saturdays at 5:00pm. Central Time.

❑   Admission: Park Admission $5.00. Individual tickets for rides or all-day Armband for most activities $15.00.

❑   Miscellaneous: Year-round full service campground, party rooms.

This is actually a multi-purpose facility offering entertainment in car racing (stock and NHRA dragsters) and the improved amusement park featuring adult and kiddie rides. The smaller scale amusement park is easily family-friendly with rides like go-carts, bumper cars, merry-go-round, giant slide, Tilt-A-Whirl, Big Mac Truck ride, Western Train ride, Tornado, Fire House Fun Land, Flying Dragon Roller Coaster, Deluxe Sizzler, Dizzy Dragon, Jitter Bug, mini-golf, a water slide, flume ride and swimming pool. Wet, dry, fast or slow - you guys decide what kind of day you're in the mood for.

BRIMS - BARREN RIVER IMAGINATIVE MUSEUM OF SCIENCE

1229 Center Street (Downtown)

Bowling Green 42101

- ❑ Phone: (270) 843-9779. **Web: www.premiernet.net/~brims**
- ❑ Hours: Thursday-Saturday 10:00am-3:00pm, Sunday 1:00pm-4:00pm. Closed holidays. Central Time.
- ❑ Admission: $2.50-$3.50 per person.

"Learn the secrets to over 30 fascinating hands-on exhibits". The BRIMS Blaster is a mini-tornado, the van de Graaf Electrostatic Generator can be "hair-raising", operating a giant interactive model railroad is easy, the wind tunnel measures air flow and you can suspend your body with the help of Magic Mirrors. Learning and fun combined at a reasonable price.

LOST RIVER CAVE AND VALLEY

Corner of Nashville Road, (31W) & Cave Mill Road (I-65 take Exit 20 onto William Natcher Parkway, travel 4 miles to Exit #4 (31W)

Bowling Green 42101

- ❑ Phone: (270) 393-0077 or (866) 274-CAVE
  Web: www.lostrivercave.com
- ❑ Hours: Daily 10:00am-5:00pm (April-October). except Thanksgiving, Christmas and New Year's. Group tours available by reservation (call for details). Boat tours during winter months and inclement weather are subject to cancellation. Central Time.
- ❑ Admission: $11.50 adult, $10.50 senior (65+), $6.50 child (6-12), $1.50 preschooler.
- ❑ Tours: Tours leave at the top of each hour beginning at 10:00am and ending at 4:00pm.

The only floating cave tour in Kentucky, it's also "re-found" and run by some very enthusiastic, fun folks. Right under the street is a cave with a river that "Ripley's Believe It or Not" has claimed is the shortest, and deepest river in the world. You'll begin with the walking, history and nature portion of the tour. The cave and valley dates back over 10,000 years ago when it provided shelter at

For updates visit our website: www.kidslovepublications.com

one time or another for Native Americans, both Confederate and Union soldiers and the notorious Jesse James and his gang after they had robbed the bank in nearby Russellville. You'll also see a "Blue Hole" freak of nature for yourself and hear the mysterious stories surrounding those who fall in it. As you come to the cave's entrance, everyone will want to explore the giant dance floor in the popular underground big band nightclub from the 30's and 40's. Now, your group will board a long boat and the guide will use only their hand-held light to venture into the cave. It's a small test of nerves as you go deeper into the cave, but the guide is careful to keep the mood "light" and talkative. An adventure not to be missed by your family!

NATIONAL CORVETTE MUSEUM

350 Corvette Drive (I-65, exit 28)

Bowling Green 42101

❑   Phone: (800) 53-VETTE. **Web: www.corvettemuseum.com**
❑   Hours: Daily 8:00am-5:00pm. Closed only Thanksgiving and
     Christmastime. Central Time.
❑   Admission: $8.00 adult, $6.00 senior (55+), $4.50 child (6-16),
     $20.00 family.

What a great way to further enhance your visit to the Corvette Factory! Especially designed for Corvette enthusiasts, you will be treated to thousands of Corvette-related exhibits and more than 50 models of every vintage, including the coveted 1953 Corvette (one of only 300 produced). You will especially love the concept cars (cars that were tested in design, but not ever produced for sale). The Chevrolet Theatre sets the stage with a high energy film about this special car. Experience the romance that has lasted over 50 years in the Nostalgia Area. Full-scale exhibits include: The Barbershop, A 1960's Service Station, 1960's Dealer Showroom, and "Route 66" which explores the feeling of spending a day with your Corvette on the open road. The Performance Area highlights the racing success of Team Corvette. Kids will love the Design and Concept Area that teaches how cars are first designed in clay through final production. Be sure to bring your camera for some great "car and driver" shots. Note: A great virtual tour is on the website.

RUSSELL SIMS AQUATIC CENTER

2303 Tomblinson Way (at Preston S. Miller Park off of Veterans Memorial Blvd.)

Bowling Green 42101

❏ Phone: (270) 393-3271
   Web: www.bgky.org/bgpr/aquatics.htm
❏ Hours: Daily 11:00am-7:30pm. Sunday open at 1:00pm. Central Time.
❏ Admission: $8.00 adult, $5.00 senior and youth (6-17), $3.00 child (2-5). Twilight Fee (after 4:30pm) 1/2 price.
❏ Miscellaneous: No outside food or drink allowed in the pool facility. Toddlers must wear swim diapers.

A newer community facility features a stainless steel 50-meter swimming pool, a zero-depth entry area with interactive water play structures like palm trees, tumble buckets and tea cups. Kids will love the splash playground full of water squirting toys such as a teeter totter, water cannons, spiral spray, water trikes and spray balls. The center also features a butterfly slide, spiral water tunnel, two double water slides and a concession area. Splash In!

WESTERN KENTUCKY UNIVERSITY

1400 Kentucky Street. Planetarium on State Street. (I-65 exit 28. Follow 31-W to Western Kentucky University)

Bowling Green 42101

❏ Phone: (270) 745-2592. **Web: www.wku.edu/library/museum**
❏ Hours: Tuesday-Saturday 9:30am-4:00pm, Sunday 1:00-4:00pm. These are times for museum only. Central time.
❏ Admission: $2.00 general (age 5+). FREE on Sundays. These are fees for museum only. All facilities are closed during holidays and school breaks.

Within the walls of the museum are the Felts Log House; Main Street: Mirror of Change; Growing up Victorian: A Kentucky Childhood; and, First American Roads, Rails and Rivers: Warren County Then and Now. There's a wide assortment of prehistoric objects, pioneer relics, old fashioned toys and musical instruments.

```
         Barnes & Noble Bookseller
           4100 Summit Plaza Drive
            Louisville, KY 40241
                502-327-0410
    502-327-0410 02-19-05 S02196 R008

CUSTOMER RECEIPT COPY

PEACE / VARIOUS                    15.99
724347677328
DISCOUNT         16.99 - 1.00
Little Princess / Ws              14.99
085391910022
Kids Love Kentucky: A Pa          13.95
097268543X


SUB TOTAL                         44.93
SALES TAX                          2.70
TOTAL                             47.63
AMOUNT TENDERED
AMEX                              47.63
CARD #:              ***********3008
AMOUNT              47.63
AUTH CODE           594353


TOTAL PAYMENT                     47.63
       Thank You for shopping at
       Barnes & Noble Booksellers
#61418  02-19-05 02:11P NW
```

PEACE / VARIOUS   18.99
724347577321
DISCOUNT   16.99 – 1.00
Little Princess / Ks   14.99
083391510022
Kids Love Kentucky / Fa   13.95
0972685434

CARD #   ************XXXX
AMOUNT   47.83
AUTH CODE   049393

TOTAL PAYMENT   47.63
Thank You for shopping at
Barnes & Noble Booksellers

Hardin Planetarium has a 40-foot dome housing a star projector, special effects projectors with show times on Tuesdays and Thursdays at 7:30pm and Sundays at 2:30pm. Call (270) 745-4044 for exact show times and info. Listen for the Cherry Hall Carillon chimes in the symbolic dome on campus.

CAPITOL ARTS CENTER
416 East Main Street
Bowling Green 42104

❑   Phone: (270) 782-ARTS. **Web: www.capitolarts.com**

Their·family series performances are based on popular elementary school-aged literature.

CORVETTE ASSEMBLY PLANT
Louisville Road & Corvette Drive (I-65 exit 28)
Bowling Green 42104

❑   Phone: (270) 745-8419
    Web: www.bowlinggreenassemblyplant.com
❑   Admission: FREE
❑   Tours: Guided, Monday-Friday 9:00am and 1:00pm. No cameras
    or purses/pouches allowed. Closed holidays, month of December
    and the first two weeks in July. Required age 7+. Closed-toe
    shoes required. Central Time.

Since 1953, people have been drawn to the mystic powers that only comes from America's true sports car...the Corvette. This 2 seat legend has been produced here for worldwide distribution since 1982. We were absolutely amazed at the careful planning and "close-up" experiences that you'll get from this walking (1-mile) factory tour. Begin your tour with an introductory film and then see photos from famous owners from all over the world in the gallery. You'll also have a chance to win Corvette souvenirs in a trivia contest while you're waiting for your tour to begin. *(Hint: The only year a Corvette was not produced was 1983)*. Once on your tour, your heads will be spinning in all directions seeing body panels being assembled and welding robots in action. Then see "the body marriage" where the newly created body meets the frame, suspension components, and its "heart"... the powerful V-8 engine. Maybe Mom or Dad will even get to start and drive a newly produced car off the line! The final highlight is watching the newly produced cars (18 per hour) enter a special glass enclosed booth for acceleration and braking tests. Hear the car's engine growl to life and quickly accelerate to nearly 100 miles per hour and then come to a screeching halt. The car's tires spin specially made wheels in the floor which are connected to computers that measure all of the performance specifications. Aaah...if Corvette would only make a mini-van!

FLOYD COLLINS STORY OUTDOOR DRAMA

Green River Amphitheatre (I-65 exit 38, to Rt. 101 that turns into Rt. 259, watch for signs)

Brownsville 42210

- ❑   Phone: (270) 597-2703 or (800) 624-8687
- ❑   Shows: Call for dates and times each season. Generally performances every Friday and Saturday night at 8:00pm. Last weekend in June through Labor Day weekend.
- ❑   Admission charged.

Come see the story of a man trapped in a cave for 16 days in the early 1900's plus other folktale productions. The Floyd Collins production dramatizes the life of Floyd Collins, a Kentucky farmer, whose story about being trapped in Sand Cave (near Mammoth Cave) for two weeks captivated the entire country in 1926. Charles Lindberg, then an unknown mail pilot, and William "Skeets" Miller, who won a Pulitzer Prize for his coverage of the ordeal, are just a part of this tragedy which dramatizes the nationwide effort to free Collins before it is too late.

SC – South Central Area 79

DALE HOLLOW LAKE STATE RESORT PARK

6371 State Park Road (I-65 exit 43 or 53. KY 90 east, then south on KY 449 & KY 1206),

Burkesville 42717

❑ Phone: (270) 433-7431 or (800) 325-2282
  Web: www.state.ky.us/agencies/parks/dalehol.htm
❑ Miscellaneous: Eagle Watch Weekends (last two of January). Join other eagle watchers on open barge tours to view the bald eagle in its natural wintering habitat. Admission for programs & tours.

On a bluff overlooking a 28,000 acre lake, the modern lodge offers extreme comfort in a wilderness setting. There's great fishing, boating, swimming, hiking trails, horseback riding and mountain biking. There's also a campground, marina and a pool at the lodge.

GENERAL BURNSIDE ISLAND STATE PARK

PO Box 488 (US 27, 8 miles south of Somerset)

Burnside 42517

❑ Phone: (606) 561-4104 or (606) 561-4192
  Web: www.state.ky.us/agencies/parks/genburns.htm

During the Civil War, Union General Ambrose Burnside and his troops patrolled this island to keep watch for Confederate soldiers. General Burnside has gone down in history for his beard and moustache worn with clean-shaven chin - called a "burnsider"; now called a "sideburn". The Island Park is surrounded by Lake Cumberland. Most like the park for camping, fishing and boating. There's also a pool and recreation programs.

GREEN RIVER LAKE STATE PARK

179 Park Office Road (KY 55)

Campbellsville 42718

❑ Phone: (270) 465-8255
  Web: www.state.ky.us/agencies/parks/greenriv.htm

This land is where Confederate General John Hunt Morgan was captured after the Battle of Tebbs Band in 1863. The Atkinson

Griffin House was the hospital set up for the defeated Confederates and now houses a battle diorama, weaponry, slide show and exhibits (Visitor's Center). Other amenities are the shoreline campground, beach, mini-golf, 20 miles of hiking trails and mountain biking. There's also a marina with rental boats.

BIG MIKE'S MYSTERY HOUSE

566 Old Mammoth Cave Rd (I-65 exit 53, Hwy. 70 W, straight on Hwy 235 @ Big Mike's Rock & Gift Shop)

Cave City 42127

❑   Phone: (270) 773-5144
     Web: www.mammothcave.com/bigmikes.htm
❑   Hours: Open daily (except winter) at 9:00am. Closing times are seasonal. Central Time.
❑   Small Admission charged.
❑   Miscellaneous: Kentucky's largest rock shop with gifts, toys and souvenirs.

Feel the force of gravity in a strange and mysterious way. See the old dinosaur skull.

CRYSTAL ONYX CAVE

8709 Happy Valley Rd (off I-65 exit 53 east on KY 90)

Cave City 42127

❑   Phone: (270) 773-2359
❑   Hours: Daily 8:00am-6:00pm (Memorial Day –Labor Day), Open from 9:00am-5:00pm rest of year. Closed January. Central time.
❑   Admission: $4.00-$6.00 (age 5+).
❑   Miscellaneous: Campground with 25 primitive sites, 25 improved sites.

Crystal Onyx Cave has a variety of beautiful formations such as delicate crystalline draperies and rimstone pools. The guided one-hour tour includes a pre-historic burial site.

DINOSAUR WORLD

711 Mammothcave Road (I-65 exit 53)

Cave City 42127

❑   Phone: (270) 773-4345.   **Web: www.dinoworld.net**
❑   Hours: Daily 8:30am-sunset (March-October). Other seasons,
    weather pending (call for seasonal closing times).
❑   Admission: $8.00-$10.00 (age 3+).
❑   Miscellaneous: Picnic areas and gift shop.

Take an outdoor step back in time viewing over 100 life-size
dinosaurs. Want some questions answered about the dinos (like,
are all these figures really dinosaurs, or something else)? They
really try to educate here, too.

FLOYD COLLINS MUSEUM

1240 Old Mammoth Cave Road (KY 70, Wayfarer Bed & Breakfast)

Cave City 42127

❑   Phone: (270) 773-3366
    Web: www.mammothcave.com/wayfare.htm
❑   Hours: Daytime, Central Time.

Near the entrance to Mammoth Cave park, it was originally an
early 1930's souvenir shop. While exploring Sand Cave in 1925,
Floyd Collins caught his leg. They attempted rescue, but couldn't.
His death was the most widely reported news events of that time.
The museum is housed in a bed & breakfast.

GUNTOWN MOUNTAIN

SR 90 (I-65 exit 53, then SRKY 70 west)

Cave City 42127

❑   Phone: (270) 773-3530
    Web: www.mammothcave.com/guntown/
❑   Hours: Daily 9:00am-8:00pm, Memorial day-Labor Day.
    Weekends only 10:00am-6:00pm (May, September -
    mid-October). All times are Central Time.

❑   Admission: $15.95 day pass to everything on site (age 5+). Cave tours are $5.00 adult, $3.00 child. $9.95 adult and $5.95 child (5-11) for Town and Chair lift (Kiddie Rides and games separate).

❑   Miscellaneous: Saloon Snack Bar eatery, gift shops.

"Howdie" - it's a recreated 1880's frontier town amusement park. The town performs gun fights, a magic show, country music shows, and cancan shows (with funny antics) throughout the day. Begin your day with chair lift rides to the top of the mountain (or take shuttle bus) where the activity is. The gun fights appear to be real western shootouts with up to nine gunfights daily - each one staged differently. You never know who the bad guys are until the story unfolds. A half-hour cave tour of onyx cave is available as well as kiddie rides including a giant Ferris wheel overlooking the city. Before you leave, be sure to pay to have someone locked in the town jail ($1.00 for 5 minutes). Contact the sheriff.

KENTUCKY ACTION PARK AND JESSE JAMES RIDING STABLES

3057 Mammoth Cave Road (I-65 exit 53 to Hwy. 70 west)

Cave City 42127

❑   Phone: (270) 773-2560 or (800) 798-0560
      Web: www.mammothcave.com/kyaction.htm

❑   Admission: Based on activity. Several dollars per person/per activity.

Play the western themed mini-golf course or ride the favorite alpine slide for a thrilling quarter of a mile. Then, watch on-site glass-blowing as you lick your ice cream cone or roast a hot dog or marshmallow at the fire pit. After your snack, ride the bumper boats or exciting go cart rides. Many who visit comment that their horse riding trails are fun and well lead by guides - good for that early horseback riding experience.

MAMMOTH CAVE JELLYSTONE PARK CAMP RESORT

1002 Mammoth Cave Rd (3 miles from the Mammoth Cave entrance), **Cave City** 42127

❑ Phone: (270) 773-3840 or (800) 523-1854
   Web: www.jellystonemammothcave.com
❑ Season: Mid-April - October. Rental Fees for accommodations are $50-$100 per night with $30 fee for campsites. Most planned activities are free with stay. Large slide, mini-golf and some other more supervised play areas require a small fee.
❑ Miscellaneous: Joe's Diner is an old fashioned 1950's style restaurant serving "grill kitchen" breakfasts and sandwich lunches. Open at 7:00am. Camp store, laundry, ice, propane, RV supplies, fast food snack shop and gift shop.

The offerings at the largest resort park in Kentucky include: Daily visits by Yogi, Boo-Boo and Cindy; a large swimming pool with toddler pool; 350' waterslide; Yogi's petting zoo; arts and crafts; outdoor movies/bonfires; music synthesizer, mini-golf; game room; bank shot basketball; beach volleyball; small rides; batting cages; athletic fields; hiking trails; hayrides.

MAMMOTH CAVE WAX MUSEUM

SRKY 90 (I-65 exit 53)

Cave City 42127

❑ Phone: (270) 773-3010
   Web: www.mammothcave.com/wax.htm
❑ Hours: Daily 9:00am-9:00pm (summer), Daily 9:00am-5:00pm (March-May & September/October). Central Time.
❑ Admission: $6.00 adult, $5.00 senior (60+), $3.00 child (4-12).
❑ Miscellaneous: Next door is Huckleberry Hill Village with mini-golf, bumper cars and shopping.

Not just 120 wax figures, but remarks are listed by each display. Mostly early heroes and statesmen or great stars like Albert Einstein, Abraham Lincoln, M.L. King, Elvis, Walt Disney and Jesus. Which hero is your favorite?

MAMMOTH CAVE WILDLIFE MUSEUM

SR 90 (I-65 exit 53, east on SRKY 90)

Cave City 42127

☐ Phone: (270) 773-2255
   Web: www.mammothcave.com/wildlife.htm
☐ Hours: Daily 9:00am-8:00pm (March-October). Weekends only (November-February). Central Time.
☐ Admission: $6.00 adult, $3.00 child (3-11).

Here they have a collection of wildlife specimens from around the world - all mounted in scenes that resemble their natural surroundings. The white, cave-like hallways wind to and fro. Each of the 1600 stuffed wildlife are clean, beautiful and crisp. Look for our favorites: the reindeer, giant moose, lobster, porcupine, Kodiak bear and giant Polar Bear. This is the nicest, freshest wildlife museum we've visited in our multi-state travel.

WIGWAM VILLAGE

601 North Dixie Hwy. (I-65 exit 53 to SRKY90 to US 31W north)

Cave City 42127

☐ Phone: (270) 773-3381 **Web: www.wigwamvillage.com**
☐ Hours: March - November. Central Time Zone.
☐ Rates: Reasonable, most around $50.00 per night. Close to Mammoth Cave and Kentucky Down Under.
☐ Miscellaneous: Heat and A/C, private bath, tile floor, no pets, TV w/ cable, gift shop, in-room coffee. Families should request rooms with two beds or rent two teepees (or plan to camp out on the floor of the bedroom). Grills and picnic shelter outside.

"Sleep in a Wigwam!". 15 actual wigwams (a name for permanent teepees) for overnight stay. The dream of a man in the mid-1930's, they have become national treasures. This location is one of only two left open in the United States. Check in at the 52 foot tall center teepee and gift shop. The gift shop has cute ceramic teepees that look just like your room for the night (be sure to purchase one as a souvenir of your stay - get one with your room number painted on it). The rooms are quaintly small and furnished with original hickory and cane furniture. Without the distraction of a telephone, you can meet your wigwam neighbors at the gathering place in the middle with a playground and Misting Deck to cool off on hot summer days. Definitely a great place to tell the folks at home about!

MCDOWELL HOUSE AND APOTHECARY

125 South 2nd Street, downtown

Danville 40422

❑   Phone: (859) 236-2804. Web: www.mcdowellhouse.com

❑   Hours: Monday-Saturday 10:00am-Noon & 1:00-4:00pm.
    Sunday 2:00-4:00pm. Closed Monday (November-February).
    Closed Thanksgiving, Christmas and winter Mondays.

❑   Admission: $5.00 adult, $3.00 senior (62+), $2.00 youth (13-20),
    $1.00 child (1-12).

❑   Tours: Guided 45 minute tours.

❑   Miscellaneous: Gardens with medicinal herbs. Stop over at
    Constitution Square across the street.

This medical office is a showcase to one of the world's finest collections of antique apothecary jars and equipment (did you know they used to hide medicine in biscuit dough as the coating?). Danville is the boyhood and adult home of Dr. Ephraim McDowell - the man who performed the world's first successful abdominal surgery. Jane Todd Crawford, the patient, thought she was pregnant and overdue. After diagnosing a growing ovarian tumor, McDowell suggested her only hope for survival was to travel 60 miles (on horseback) to his office. After writing a prayer in his journal, he performed the experimental removal on Christmas Day, 1809, while Mrs. Crawford sang hymns. She fully recovered, went home to her family, and lived into her 70s. Just a few of the many very unique items you need to look for are: the clock in the foyer with an arrow hole through it; the cradle that rocks and rolls; the comb-back rocker (if you have long hair you might be chosen to demo this); the little door into the "operating bedroom" with the doctor's tools laid out on the chest of drawers; in the kitchen, an old-fashioned deep fryer (french fries) or "toe" stir (toaster); or why a green jar was always placed within view of the apothecary window. We promise you'll see something here (esp. medically) you've never seen before! Very, very interesting.

PIONEER PLAYHOUSE
840 Stanford Road (US 150)
Danville 40422

- ❑ Phone: (859) 236-2747. Web: www.pioneerplayhouse.com
- ❑ Hours: Dinner served 7:30pm. Show time 8:30pm. Mid-June to Mid-August. Performances Nightly Tuesday through Saturday.
- ❑ Admission: Reserved Seats with Dinner & Theatre: around $20.00 (children under 6: $6.50). Theatre Only: around $12.00 (children under 6: $3.50)

Operating since the 1950's, this is a rustic style outdoor dinner theatre (in case of rain, indoors). The complex of wooden beam buildings serve as pioneer shops and eateries. Plus, each building tells a unique story about Kentucky history. Seasonally, they perform 5 different plays - usually two of them are rated G - for family audiences (ex. All I Really Need to Know I Learned in Kindergarten or Sherlock Holmes).

OLD JAIL & JAILER'S QUARTERS
206 North College Street (downtown)
Franklin 42135

- ❑ Phone: (270) 586-4228
- ❑ Hours: Monday-Friday 9:00am-4:00pm, Saturday 10:00am-2:00pm. Central time.

The county's archives are here, but, most probably come to see the graffiti and drawings by Civil War soldiers held in these jailer's quarters. A glimpse at what pioneer justice was like.

PENN'S STORE

257 Penn's Store Road (Junction of SRKY 37 and SRKY 243),
(across the creek/concrete bridge)
Gravel Switch 40328

❑   Phone: (859) 332-7715. **Web: www.PennsStore.com**

❑   Hours: Wednesday, Thursday, Saturday & Sunday 10:00am-
5:00pm. Weekday afternoons perchance. Their hours are
"country hours" which means "give or take" a few minutes.

❑   Admission: FREE

❑   Miscellaneous: Herbal Gardens and product, Books on History of
Penn's Store, Penn's Store Family Cookbook, Penn's official
souvenirs, candies, homemade dolls.

A store site since 1845, in the Penn family since 1850. Penn's
Store is the oldest country store in America in continuous
operation and ownership by the same family. This is where the 1st
post office originated on November 7, 1882 with the postmark
reading, "Rollings, Kentucky" - see some memorabilia from those
earlier postal years. Inside, the floor and shelves sag a little here
and there. Notice the old style countertops and glass showcases or
the cigar box used as a cash register. On cold days, the wood/coal
stove in the middle of the store provides warmth and entices you to
"sit a spell". Chances are you'll meet some locals actually
shopping like their pioneer ancestors did for generations (we met
the neighbor lady up the street). See Penn's Privy - it received
national attention in 1992 when the first restroom facilities were
installed on the site. Impromptu entertainment can stir up at any
moment - whittlers, fiddlers, musicians, story tellers and singers
are always stopping by to share their talents. One promise, this
place will still seem unbelievable, even after you've been there!
That's the word - unbelievable.

GREENSBURG BOTTLING COMPANY

108 South Depot Street, **Greensburg** 42743

❑   Phone: (270) 932-5061. **Web: www.doublecolaski.com**

❑   Admission: FREE

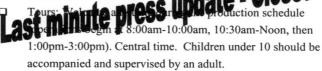

❑   Tours: ~~Varies~~ ... ...production schedule ...begin at 8:00am-10:00am, 10:30am-Noon, then 1:00pm-3:00pm). Central time. Children under 10 should be accompanied and supervised by an adult.

A small, family-owned soft drink bottling operation which produces "Ski", a soft drink made famous by the Kentucky Headhunters and their Grammy-award winning song, "Dumas Walker." Visitors can see a historic bottling operation still producing returnable bottles (watch the bottles being filled, capped and cased). Most of all, children like the free drink offered at the end of the tour.

HIDDEN RIVER CAVE AND THE AMERICAN CAVE MUSEUM

119 East Main Street (I-65 exit 58, Rte. 218 east)

Horse Cave 42749

❑   Phone: (270) 786-1466. **Web: www.cavern.org**

❑   Hours: Daily 9:00am-5:00pm. Open 'til 7:00pm during the summer. Central time.

❑   Admission: $8.00 adult, $4.00 child (5-13) for museum and cave. $4.00 museum only.

❑   Tours: Guided cave tours leave each hour from the museum. Tours may depart more frequently during the summer season.

"Visit the Incredible" and descend over 100 feet below the surface of the earth. Along with rushing underground water and odd-shaped structures common with caves in the area, there's also underground ruins of an 1890's era hydroelectric system. Hear the stories of how the cave was saved from pollution to become a model for conservation. The American Cave Museum is a showcase of exhibits about prehistoric cave explorers, modern cave spelunkers, cave lighting, and the story of the "Kentucky Cave Wars" (some of the funny things owners would do to attract tourists and some of the sad things that happened for the sake of exploration). Learn about groundwater science and conservation, mining and finally, a wonderful gallery of American Caves. The cave may look like others in the region but the museum is professionally done and covers all American caves - a nice add-on feature of this visit.

KENTUCKY DOWN UNDER / KENTUCKY CAVERNS

SR 235 (I-65 exit 58 to KY 235 east)

Horse Cave 42749

❑ Phone: (270) 786-2634 or (800) 762-2869. **Web: www.kdu.com**
❑ Hours: Daily 8:00am-5:00pm (mid-March thru October).
Kentucky Caverns remain open the rest of the year 9:00am-4:00pm. Closed Thanksgiving, New Year's Day and Christmas. All times are Central Time.
❑ Admission: Regular season (mid-March - October) $18.75 adult, $16.87 senior (62+), $10.50 child (5-14). Admission rest of year: $10.95 adult, $9.86 senior, $6.95 child.
❑ Miscellaneous: Gift shops. Most walkways are paved.

This wonderful interactive nature park helps you experience Australian wildlife. Have you ever touched a kangaroo? (Discovery Area); fed a baby lamb by bottle or watched Border Collies herd sheep - you'll hear "Away" & "That'll Do" just like in "Babe" (Woolshed); learned to toss a boomerang or danced to the Aborigines Welcome song or learned circular breathing to play the rhythms of the didgeridoo? (Corroboree); journeyed thru an ancient underground passage? (Kentucky Caverns - 45 minute tours); looked at "frogmouth birds" up close?; tasted a bison burger and other "Aussie" favorites? (Outback Café open weekends or daily in the summer); walked among emus and wallabies with Joeys? (Land Down Under Walkabout); or walked in an aviary where exotic birds feed as they land on your arm, shoulder or head? (Lorikeet Flight Cage). Wow, what an unforgettable family day! Please don't forget your cameras here.

LAKE CUMBERLAND STATE RESORT PARK

5465 State Park Road (I-65, exit Cumberland Parkway to US 127 or I-75 exit KY80)

Jamestown 42629

❑   Phone: (270) 343-3111 (lodge), (800) 325-1709, (888) 782-8336.
Web: www.state.ky.us/agencies/parks/lakecumb.htm

This Park is known throughout the region as one of the finest fishing and pleasure boating areas in the Eastern United States. The Lure Lodge has an indoor swimming pool with exercise room and hot tub and the smaller Pumpkin Creek Lodge is peaceful and quiet. Also available are Wildwood Cottages in the woods, nature trails, horseback riding, campground, marina, rental boats, a beach, tennis, mini-golf and recreation programs. Other points of interest in the area are the Russell Springs Visitor Center (270) 866-4333, Waterway Adventures (800) 844-8862 or www.waterway-adventures.com, Wolf Creek Dam Visitor Center (off US 27, open weekdays) and Wolf Creek National Fish Hatchery (US 127 below dam, 7:00am-3:30pm daily).

HOOFPRINTS ON THE STAIRS

370 N Spalding Avenue (Myrtledene, Center Square Grounds)

Lebanon 40033

❑   Phone: (270) 692-6002. **Web: www.hoofprintsonthestairs.com**
❑   Hours: 2 weekends in August.
❑   Admission: $4.00 to $9.00 per person (age 6+).
❑   Miscellaneous: Bring lawn chairs and blankets.

A Civil War musical drama depicting Lebanon's role in the War, held in August only on the grounds of Myrtledene. Built in 1833, this Victorian home was headquarters for General John Hunt Morgan who, in July 1862, once rode his horse up the stairs. Designated a Kentucky landmark.

BARREN RIVER LAKE STATE PARK RESORT

1149 State Park Rd (I-65 to the Cumberland Pkwy, then US 31 E south), **Lucas** 42156

❑ Phone: (270) 646-2151 Lodge, (800) 325-0057 reservations, (270) 646-2357 Marina.
Web: www.state.ky.us/agencies/parks/barren.htm

The gently rolling hills of trees now cover the "barren" days when pioneers came to the area and found all vegetation burned away by Indians to promote grassland for grazing buffalo. The lodge, full-service restaurant and cottages curve around the 10,000 acre lake with ample fishing, boating, horseback riding, swimming (pool & beach), hiking, tennis and caving nearby.

MAMMOTH CAVE NATIONAL PARK

(I-65 exit 53 OR I-65 exit 48, follow signs)

Mammoth Cave 42259

❑ Phone: (270) 758-2328 or (800) 967-2283
Web: www.nps.gov/maca

❑ Hours: Visitor Center 7:30am-7:00pm (Summers). 8:00am-6:00pm (Fall/Spring). 8:00am-5:00pm (Winter, except 9:00am-5:00pm January-mid-February). Closed on Christmas. Central Time.

❑ Admission: Average Prices are $7.00-8.00 adult, $4.00 senior, $4.00-5.00 child (6-12)

❑ Miscellaneous: Surface Programs - like Sand Cave Almanac with cave exploring, trip to Floyd Collins family homeplace - walk in the footsteps of tragedy. Evening Programs - 8:15pm - like Myth & Mysteries of the Underworld - discussion of ancient and modern cave myths. Miss Green River II - one hour riverboat tour - wind between high limestone cliffs and pass cave entrances. 4-6 cruises daily, April-October. (270) 758-2243. Moderate admission charged for cruises. Tickets at Visitor Center. Also fishing, boating, trails, lodging, cottages, camping and horseback riding.

Mammoth Cave National Park (cont.)

Native Americans discovered Mammoth Cave about 4000 years ago and late 1700 settlers rediscovered the cave. By the War of 1812, slaves mined saltpeter from caves to be used to make gunpowder. The park was officially established in 1941. There are two worlds to explore - the underground and the surface world of tall-treed forests, rivers and wildlife (you'll probably see a wild turkey or deer cross your path on the way in). Mammoth Cave is claimed to be the longest cave system discovered on earth - over 350 miles charted on 5 levels! On tour, it's promised you'll learn something new. Did you know the science behind cave formations? Carbonic acid is what forms the rock (the same ingredient as in colas you drink!). Be on the lookout for troglodytes - animals adapted exclusively to darkness. Some tours lead to the Snowball Room where there's an underground picnic area. Advance tour tickets may be purchased by phone or web and then picked up at the Visitors Center at least 30 minutes before tour departure. There are gobs of people there and on a summer weekday practically every popular tour is sold out. Please make advance reservations. Plan to spend one-half to a full day here. Concessions and dining are available. With reasonable prices, try to take advantage of at least two activities. The most popular tours are listed below:

❑   THE HISTORIC TOUR - (2 miles, 2 hours). Emphasis on: Large trunk passages; oldest tour routes; cultural history. Best for school-aged kids who can walk for almost 2 hours. $5.00-$10.00 per person.

❑   THE FROZEN NIAGARA TOUR - (3/4 mile, 2 hours). Emphasis on: Deep pits; high domes; dry cave passages; dripstone area at exit; dynamic cave being carved by water; animal life. Good for 1st long cave tour. $5.00-$10.00 per person.

❑   THE TRAVERTINE TOUR - (1/4 mile, 1 ¼ hours). Emphasis On: Formation of cave; development of dripstone; animal life. Less strenuous version of Frozen Niagara Tour with only half sites visited. Best for young ones - probably too short and boring for older kids. $4.50-$9.00 per person.

MILL SPRINGS BATTLEFIELD
KY 80W
Nancy 42544

❑   Phone: (606) 679-1859. **Web: www.millsprings.net**
❑   Hours: Dawn to dusk. Best to tour on weekends.
❑   Admission: FREE
❑   Miscellaneous: Gift shop open weekends esp. during the summer.

Nearby in Monticello, Mill Springs Park where an 1840 mill still grinds cornmeal powered by a 40 foot overshot wheel. Open daily 9:00am-5:00pm,. Demos on weekends at 2:00pm (Memorial Day-Labor Day). (606) 368-8189.

Pick up the 9 stop driving or walking tour brochure as you enter the property. This is the site of the 1862 Civil War battle where Confederate General Zollicoffer fell and 203 soldiers died. See both Union and Confederate cemeteries, the area where infantry formed for bayonet charges, and the site of the Confederate field hospital.

DIAMOND CAVERNS
Rt. 255, 1900 Mammoth Cave Pkwy (I-65 exit 48)
Park City 42160

❑   Phone: (270) 749-2233. **Web: www.diamondcaverns.com**
❑   Hours: Open year-round. Central Time. Closed only Christmas & Thanksgiving Days. 9:00am-5:00pm (until 6:00pm Summer).
❑   Admission: $12.00 adult, $6.00 child (4-12).
❑   Tours: ½ mile long, guided. Tours leave every 30 minutes, daily.
❑   Miscellaneous: Gift shop, dining in the Brass Lantern Restaurant Café.

This cave has been open since 1859 and is known for its state-of-the-art lighting of the live calcite formations. As in many caverns, there's a Rotunda Room with "the Onyx Haystack" and lots of geological insight presented by the guide.

PERRYVILLE BATTLEFIELD STATE HISTORIC SITE

1825 Battlefield Road
(US 68 west to US 150 west to SRKY 1920 north)

Perryville 40468

❑   Phone: (859) 332-8631
    Web: www.kystateparks.com/agencies/parks/perryvil.htm
❑   Hours: Park open year-round 9:00am-9:00pm. Museum: 9:00am-
    5:00pm (April-October). By appointment (November-March).
❑   Admission: $1.00-$2.00 per person (age 6+).
❑   Miscellaneous: Picnicking, Gift Shop.

"I think to lose Kentucky is nearly the same as to lose the whole
game...", says Lincoln.   On October 8, 1862 the tranquil
countryside of the area was thundered by cannon explosions and
the death of more than 6000 killed, wounded, or missing. The
Confederate Cemetery is where many were buried by neighbors
and farmers in mounds.   Perryville became the site of the most
destructive Civil War battle in the state.   The Museum tells the
details of the battle that was the south's last serious attempt to gain
possession of Kentucky.   They use many actual maps, cannons from
battle, uniforms and weapons to tell the story.   There's also a self-
guided walking tour of the battlefield park (about one mile long).

CAVE SPRING CAVERNS

567 Rocky Hill Road (I-65 exit 38)

Smith Grove 42171

❑   Phone: (270) 563-6941
❑   Admission: $8.00 adult, $4.00 child (age 6+).
❑   Tours: Cave tours daily at 10:00am, Noon, 2:00pm and 4:00pm.
    Closed Thursdays. Central time. Tours are cancelled if there is
    excessive flooding in the area. Check first if in doubt.

Major Native American sacred site. Nature trails, bird sanctuary,
Visitor Center with art murals recreating 200-year-old Native
American artworks. Tour the cathedral size rooms & passages with
water cascades.

WILLIAM WHITLEY HOUSE STATE HISTORIC SITE

625 William Whitley Road (US 27 south to US 150 east)

Stanford 40484

❑ Phone: (606) 355-2881

❑ Hours: Tuesday-Sunday 9:00am-5:00pm (Mid-March thru December). Open Mondays in the summer. Closed Thanksgiving and Christmas.

❑ Admission: $1.00-$3.00 per person.

Mr. Whitley built the first brick house in Kentucky later named "Guardian of Wilderness Road" and had many famous visitors like George Rogers Clark and Daniel Boone. William Whitley is also noted for building the first circular track. As an expression of his anti-British sentiment, he laid his race course on clay vs. grass and ran horses counter-clockwise. While in the house, look for the concealed secret passageway used for escape should the house be invaded by Indians.

BIG SOUTH FORK NATIONAL RIVER AND RECREATION AREA

(I-75 exit 11. (SrKY92). I-65 to Cumberland Pkwy. To US 27, then KY 92 west). Get map to area from Visitor's Center.

Stearns 42647

❑ Phone: (606) 376-5073 Blue Heron. **Web: www.nps.gov/biso/**

❑ Hours: Visitors Center daily 9:00am-5:30pm (May-October). Blue Heron open 8:00am-8:00pm daily, (Summer). 8:00am-5:00pm (Rest of Year). Eastern Time.

❑ Admission: FREE

❑ Miscellaneous: Campgrounds, 150 miles of Hiking, 170 miles of Horse Trails, Picnicking, Fishing, Mountain Biking, Canoeing, Swimming, Boating. Yahoo Falls - Kentucky tallest falls accessed by car on KY 700.

The park encompasses 119,000 acres of wilderness, rivers and back country scattered with spectacular gorges and bluffs. Sparsely settled but once logged, you'll see remnants of industry. The Blue

Heron Coal Mining Camp (KY 742 off US 27 accessed by car or railroad) is a must see in the area. Within Mine 18 is the rugged and isolated life of a mining community which operated from 1938 to 1962 and employed 300 people. Recorded voices of the people who actually lived and worked in the village tell their story from inside "shell structures" representing simple homes, a church, a school, a bathhouse and a company store that even sold jewelry. The workers were paid in script, not cash, so they had to buy everything at the company store. The Tram bridge and tipple remain - also the entrance to the mine is open and an explanation of the process is given. This is a wonderfully educational, imaginative way to study the lives of miners.

BIG SOUTH FORK SCENIC RAILWAY

21 Main Street (Parkway to US 27 south to SRKY 92 west)

Stearns 42647

- ❑ Phone: (606) 376-5330 or (800) GO-ALONG
  Web: www.bsfsry.com
- ❑ Admission: $15.00 adult, $14.00 senior (60+), $7.50 child (3-12).
- ❑ Tour Departure: Wednesday, Thursday, Friday at 10:00am & 11:00am. Weekends at 11:00am and 2:30pm. In April, there's a trip on Thursday-Saturday at 10:00am & 11:00am. Added weekend trip at 10:00am (May – mid-November).
- ❑ Miscellaneous: Whistle Stop Café, Sterns Restaurant (Coal Miners Special - pinto beans and corn bread). The McCreary County Museum of history is also in this complex. The Barthell Mining Camp is an optional train ride to an old, restored mining town with an overnight in a miner's cabin (606-376-8749).

A scenic ride to Blue Heron aboard open-sided or enclosed rail cars that are pulled thru steep-walled canyons and alongside streams, pass thru a tunnel and over a bridge and into the Big South Fork River valley. Board the train at the newly restored freight warehouse (a restaurant and gift shop inside) where you can usually hear live music. The Kentucky & Tennessee Railway at one time serviced as the primary passage not only for timber and coal coming out of the valley, but also for the workers and supplies going into the coal and lumber camps. This is the best way to visit the stopover place - the Blue Heron Coal Camp.

OLD MULKEY MEETINGHOUSE STATE HISTORIC SITE

38 Old Mulkey Road (KY 1446 south off KY 100 OR KY 90 to KY 163)

Tompkinsville 42167

❑   Phone: (270) 487-8481

Web: www.state.ky.us/agencies/parks/mulkey.htm

❑   Hours: Daily 9:00am-5:00pm.

❑   Admission: FREE, self-guided tours.

Built in 1804, this is the oldest log meetinghouse in Kentucky. Many Revolutionary War soldiers and pioneers, including Daniel Boone's sister, Hannah, are buried in the church cemetery. Built during a period of religious revival, the structure has 12 corners in the shape of a cross and three doors, symbolic of the Holy Trinity.

Chapter 4
Area - South East (SE)

Our Favorites...

* Berea College Log House - Berea

* Cumberland Falls State Park Resort Park - Corbin

* Harland Sander's Cafe & Museum - Corbin

* Mountain Homeplace - Paintsville

* Bybee Pottery - Richmond

* Ft. Boonesborough State Park - Richmond

* Hummel Planterium (EKU) - Richmond

* Natural Bridge - Slade

"In Awe"
- Natural Bridge

DR. THOMAS WALKER STATE HISTORIC SITE

HC 89 Box 1868/ KY 459 (I-75 exit 29, south on US 25E)
Barbourville 40906

❑ Phone: (606) 546-4400
   Web: www.state.ky.us/agencies/parks/drwalker.htm
❑ Hours: Daily 9:00am-9:30pm

Dr. Thomas Walker was, in fact, the first frontiersman headed into Kentucky (he led the first expedition through Cumberland Gap in 1750). A physician and surveyor, he named the Cumberland and built a cabin, a replica of which stands on the site today. There's a gift shop and mini-golf on site, too.

KENTUCKY COAL MINING MUSEUM
KY 160 - Main Street, Benham 40807

❑ Phone: (606) 848-1530
   Web: www.kingdomcome.org/museum/
❑ Hours: Monday-Saturday 10:00am-5:00pm, Sunday 1:00-4:00pm. Closed Holidays.
❑ Admission: $2.50-$5.00 per person.
❑ Miscellaneous: Across the street is the School House Inn & Restaurant (606) 848-3000. Home-cooked food served in a historic coal camp school.

The building is the original coal company's commissary - now full of memorabilia from early coal mining days. Some considered camps in this area of Kentucky "Cadillac" compared to others in the coal region - mostly because miners were treated with the respect and dignity they deserved. A guided or self-guided tour gives you a feel for what it was like to live, play, and mostly, work at this unique coal camp. The museum's newest exhibit is the "Mock Mine - a short walk winding along coal corridors" with vivid sound and video from modern mines. Many like the exhibits of a typical company hospital, a typical miner's home, the mock mine and the tribute to Loretta Lynn, the "Coal Miner's Daughter" (with permission and personal artifacts from Loretta herself).

BEREA COLLEGE LOG HOUSE

College Square (I-75 exit 76)

Berea 40403

❑ Phone: (859) 985-3018 or (800) 347-3892
  Web: www.bereacollegecrafts.com
❑ Hours: Monday-Saturday 8:00am-6:00pm, Sunday 1:00-5:00pm
  (April-December). Call for winter hours.
❑ Admission: FREE
❑ Tours: Monday-Friday 10:00am and 2:00pm. 45 minutes to one
  hour long.

All students of this college work on campus in lieu of paying tuition and board - their crafts are featured at this gallery. They've been making brooms here for 80 years and weaving even longer! Visit the working studios of woodworkers (see them make the famous "Berea Basket" with all wood and paper product used), weavers (several students will make one piece - it takes two hours just to string the loom), furniture makers and broom craft (use the stalk and husk of "broom corn" - see a broom made before your eyes, then purchase it if you like). Master craftsmen supervise and teach. We were very impressed with the school's philosophies and students' attitudes about work and study! The tours are well worth the time and you'll find lots of questions to ask as you go along. Combine crafts in town with helpings of traditional Kentucky fare at Boone Tavern restaurant operated by the college's student industries since 1909. Signature items include spoonbread, Chicken Flakes in Bird's Nest (creamed chicken served in a crisp basket of fried potatoes) or maybe try some black-eyed peas, fried green tomatoes or corn pudding. The slightly formal furnishings mean children should be on their best behavior. Entrees start at $8.00 with children's portion pricing - may we suggest, lunchtime is best.

CHURCHILL WEAVERS

100 Churchill Drive
(I-75 exits 76 and 77. US 25 and Lorraine Court)

Berea 40403

❑ Phone: (859) 986-3127. **Web: www.churchill-weavers.com**

❑ Admission: FREE

❑ Tours: Self-guided Loomhouse tours Monday-Thursday 9:00am-4:00pm, Friday 9:00am-Noon (hours may vary seasonally). Closed Christmas and New Years.

Traditional loomhouse where you see the operations from warping with giant turnstile reels, weaving, to finishing with accessories. This is a large scale loomhouse. Probably the largest you'll see anywhere with 50 looms. It's like playing the drums (feet and arms move simultaneously) and sounds like horses tramping over the wooden floor.

BREAKS INTERSTATE PARK

PO Box 100 (south of Pikeville on KY/ VA 80)

Breaks 24607

❑ Phone: (540) 865-4413 or (540) 865-4414 or (800) 982-5122 **Web: www.breakspark.com**

❑ Hours: Park open 7:30am – 11:30pm except Winter when it's open until 6:00 pm. Visitor's Center open 9:00am-5:00pm seasonally.

❑ Miscellaneous: Sheltowee Trace Outfitters (800) 541-RAFT. Elkhorn Adventures Whitewater Rafting (606) 754-5080.

Sometimes called the "Grand Canyon of the South", this is the largest canyon east of the Mississippi; over 5-miles long, 1600 feet deep surrounded by sheer vertical cliffs! A paved road leads to the entrance of the canyon rim and there's a Visitor Center with natural science and historical artifacts and demos of the area's formation. Check out the park's Laurel Lake, caves, hidden springs and Russell Fork River's falls and rapids. Hiking and rafting are the name of the game here. Also within the park is a lodge, cottages, campgrounds and a pool.

BUCKHORN LAKE STATE RESORT PARK

4441 Kentucky Highway 1833 (I-64 east to the Mountain Parkway,
exit Campton and take KY 15 south to KY 28 west, then KY 1833)

Buckhorn 41721

❑   Phone: (606) 398-7510 or (606) 398-7382 (log church)
or (800) 325-0058
Web: www.state.ky.us/agencies/parks/buckhorn.htm

Getting away from it all is easy here especially for nature-lovers,
fishermen and hikers. When staying at the lodge, you can easily
hike down to Moonshiner Hollow to the 1200 acre mountain lake
below the path. Many slowly make their way down there after
dinner in the lodge or they curl up with a good book or magazine
by the copper-hooded fireplace in the lodge's lounging area.
Maybe you want to make a side trip to Buckhorn Log Church built
in 1927. Its large pipe organ and natural white oak interior make it
a man-made natural beauty too (open 9:00am-5:00pm daily).
Check out their cottages, marina, rental boats, pool, beach,
horseback riding trails and tennis and recreation programs.

MEADOWGREEN PARK BLUEGRASS MUSIC HALL

465 Forge Mill Road (I-64 exit 97 to exit 16, Rt. 15 to Rt. 42)

Clay City 40312

❑   Phone: (606) 663-9008. Web: www.chapel1.com/kfobg

26 shows of family style bluegrass music (some performed by
youth) performed in the hills.

CUMBERLAND FALLS STATE RESORT PARK

7351 State Route 90 (I-75 exit Corbin to US 25W, then to SRKY
90), Corbin 40701

❑   Phone: (606)528-4121 or (800) 325-0063 reservations
Web: www.state.ky.us/agencies/parks/cumbfal2.htm
❑   Hours: 6:00am-Midnight. Until 3:00am the 2 days before, after
and including a full moon. Eastern Time.

❑   Admission: FREE. Charge for boat rides or rentals.

❑   Tours: Rainbow Mist Ride to the Base of Falls (800) 541-7238 (mid-May thru Labor Day). Sheltowee Trace Outfitters raft trips (800) 541-RAFT.

❑   Miscellaneous: Dupont Lodge with dining, Cottages, Campground, Gift Shop, Pool, Horseback Riding, Tennis, Picnicking, Rafting.

The "Niagara of the South" is a 125 foot wide curtain of water falling 60 feet - dramatic night and day. Dawn to dusk viewing is better for photos and safety. However, it is best to visit at night when there's a full moon. Then, you hopefully will get to see the famous moonbow (arch of light and colors), a phenomena not found anywhere else in the Western Hemisphere! How outstanding and romantic (esp. for night owls)! The Museum (at lodge) features Native American artifacts and exhibits relating to plants, animals and history from the area. Eagle Falls are nearby and are a beautifully high stream of water (vs. a roaring gush). There's also a Nature Preserve and the Moonbow Trail which connects to the Daniel Boone National Forest. We find many families like to stay overnight at the lodge (very family-friendly with family activities throughout the first floor Great Room area) and wander or hike in the daytime. The Falls are within long walking distance for grade-schoolers and strollers, but there are some hills.

HARLAND SANDERS CAFÉ & MUSEUM

US 25W (I-75 exit 29, US 25E south to US 25W)

Corbin 40701

❑   Phone: (606) 528-2163

       Web: www.chickenfestival.com/sanders.htm

❑   Hours: Open daily 10:00am-10:00pm.

❑   Admission: FREE

Eat where it all began! The original Kentucky Fried Chicken Restaurant serves KFC products in the large restored dining room. See the Colonel's kitchen as it was in 1940 (early dishwashers, french fry press) when he developed his secret recipe. The business flourished because he combined good cooking, hard work and showmanship. Be sure to look in the display case for the cooking clock with the third hand. Also see his office, model motel room he rented and much of his marketing strategies. Do you know how many herbs and spices are in his chicken recipe? Did you know it was his honor system franchise concept (that he sold across country) that, at age 65+, made him money - and not his own restaurant?

KINGDOM COME STATE PARK

Box M (off US 119N)

Cumberland 40823

❑   Phone: (606) 589-2479

Web: www.state.ky.us/agencies/parks/kingdom.htm

This is Kentucky's highest state park on the crest of Pine Mountain. The park's name was taken from John Fox Jr.'s famous novel "The Little Shepherd of Kingdom Come" a book about an orphaned youth and his journey through the hills and into the Civil War. This book was the first book to sell one million copies. If you like nature, you will love seeing unusual rock formations like Log Rock, a natural sandstone bridge, and Raven Rock, a 290 foot rock at a 45-degree angle. The popular Little Shepherd Trail (Harlan to Winterburg) is recommended for hikers and slow vehicles. There's a campground, pedal boats and 5 miles of hiking trails.

ELKHORN CITY RAILROAD MUSEUM

100 Pine Street

Elkhorn City 41522

❑   Phone: (606) 754-4554

❑   Hours: Tuesday, Friday, Saturday, Sunday 9:00am-4:00pm.

❑   Admission: Donations

See how the railroad made its way into the area with photos, tools, uniforms, and instruments used on the railroad. Speak to retired railroad employees on the history of the railroad locally.

For updates visit our website: www.kidslovepublications.com

HENDERSON SETTLEMENT

KY 90 (16 miles southwest of Pineville)

Frakes 40940

❑ Phone: (606) 337-3613
❑ Hours: Craft shop Monday-Friday 8:00-4:30, Saturday by appointment.
❑ Tours: 8:30am, 10:00am, 1:00pm & 3:00pm. Prefer by appointment or as part of a mission work group.

Henderson was one of a number of settlement schools developed in rural areas, particularly in Appalachia, as a Progressive Era solution to poverty, isolation, and lack of opportunity. The schools, with boarding facilities for students whose homes were too distant for daily travel, clustered with community services, offered training for various trades, and often became laboratories for the study and preservation of local crafts and traditions. Tours of the 1,300-acre mission include the demonstration farm, with its greenhouse, orchards and vegetable gardens.

PINE MOUNTAIN SETTLEMENT

36 KY 510 (at KY 221 & KY 510)

Harlan 40831

❑ Phone: (606) 558-3571. **Web: www.kih.net/pinemountain**

Nestled in the mountains near Harlan, 800 acres of forests and fields invite you to learn folklore and the heritage of this settlement school through hands-on courses. Local mountain craftsmen help you make and take home treasures. Native stone and wood buildings provide a beautiful setting for a retreat.

HINDMAN SETTLEMENT SCHOOL
KY 160 (off KY 80 one mile)
Hindman 41822

❑   Phone: (606) 785-5475. **Web: www.hindmansettlement.org**
❑   Hours: Monday-Friday 8:00am-5:00pm
❑   Admission: FREE

Hindman Settlement School was founded in 1902 on the forks of Troublesome Creek. Folk dance evenings and workshops on Appalachian culture are offered. A 12 minute video is shown on the history of the school.

FRONTIER NURSING SERVICE
KY 80 (US 421 off Daniel Boone Pkwy.)
Hyden 41749

❑   Phone: (606) 672-2317. **Web: www.midwives.org**
❑   Hours: By Appointment.

Up until the 1930s, an American woman was more likely to die in childbirth than from any other disease, except tuberculosis. The mortality rate was particularly high for pregnant women in rural areas where hospitals and qualified medical care were scarce. Breckinridge recognized this concern and succeeded in one of the pioneering attempts to bring professionalized health care to rural-America. At the oldest school of nurse-midwifery (est. 1925) you'll see the Mary Breckenridge Hospital and nursing schools and centers.

DANIEL BOONE MOTOCROSS PARK
775 Falls City Road (I-75 exit 41, KY 80 west)
London 40741

❑   Phone: (606) 877-1364. **Web: www.danielboonemx.com**

Motocross racing and mountain bike racing with entries from many states. ATV National every April. Bike racing weekly (March-November).

LEVI JACKSON WILDERNESS ROAD STATE PARK

998 Levi Jackson Mill Road (I-75 exit 38)

London 40744

❑ Phone: (606) 878-8000
  Web: www.state.ky.us/agencies/parks/levijack.htm
❑ Hours: Park open 24 hours. Mill grounds open 8:00am-4:30pm in the summer. Museum open daily 9am-4:30pm (April-October). Everything closed the week of Christmas.
❑ Admission: up to $1.50 per person.
❑ Miscellaneous: Campground, Gift Shop, Pool (nice, w/ two water slides and a children's pool), Mini-golf, Picnicking, & Archery range.

Begin with historic trails - the Wilderness Road (30 foot wide wagon road used by pioneers) and Boone's Trace. Over 200,000 eastern settlers forged into Kentucky wilderness between 1774 and 1796 for the promise of fertile land, abundant game, clear streams and rivers. They faced many dangers - McNitt's Defeat (worst Kentucky Indian massacre) occurred here on the Wilderness Road in 1796. The Mountain Life Museum is a log building with pioneer artifacts such as kitchen utensils, weapons and furniture. At McHargue's Mill you'll see a collection of millstones which is one of the largest existing anywhere. "The people went and gathered it and ground it in mill" - Numbers 11:8.

PORTAL 31 WALKING TOUR

US 160 (2 miles east of Benham)

Lynch 40855

❑ Phone: (606) 848-1530

An outdoors tour of the 1920 coal mine and buildings. The walking tour includes the 1920 coal tipple (small-size "train conveyor" - the largest in the world at that time), the Lamp House (where miners checked in and picked up lights and mine numbers), the original post office, a depot, school, firehouse and, best of all, the mine portal entrance and actually into the mine. Built by US Steel, it was once the largest coal camp in the world with 1000+ structures.

BELL COUNTY HISTORICAL MUSEUM & COAL HOUSE

242 North 20th Street (US 25E)

Middlesboro 40965

❏ Phone: (606) 242-0005 or (800) 988-1075
   Web: www.geocities.com/bellhistorical/
❏ Hours: Museum: Monday, Wednesday & Friday 10:00am-
   2:00pm. Coal House open Monday-Friday 8:00am-4:00pm.
❏ Admission: FREE

Obviously, the focus is on coal mining. Bell County photos, artifacts and the 1926 house built out of 40 tons of bituminous coal are the main exhibits. Next door to the Coal House, an outdoor museum features coal mining equipment from the 1960s. The equipment includes a mine locomotive and coal cutting machine.

CUMBERLAND GAP NATIONAL HISTORICAL PARK

PO Box 1848 (I-75 exit US 25E south 50 miles)

Middlesboro 40965

❏ Phone: (606) 248-2817. **Web: www.nps.gov/cuga/**
❏ Hours: Visitor's Center 8:00-5:00 daily. Park open 'til dusk.
❏ Admission: FREE

Go back in time when the gap - a natural passage through the mountain barrier - had been used by Indians, and then discovered by explorer Dr. Thomas Walker. Daniel Boone and John Finley followed in 1769 - Boone and his axmen making the first Kentucky trail named the Wilderness Road. By the late 1700's, over 10,000 settlers had come west through the Cumberland Gap. The park is the largest National Historical Park in the country with over 20,000 acres. Start by viewing the orientation programs available at the Visitor Center. Look over the pictures here and then see for yourself the Pinnacle Overlook (panoramic view of three states) or Fort McCook (built by Confederate forces to guard the gap during the Civil War). A hiker's paradise - 80% of the park has unpaved roads (be sure to check the length and difficulty of trails - stick to nature trails close to paved roads for the kids). The Wilderness Road Campground has 160 campsites for tents or RVs, a restored log cabin at Martin's Fork (a Kentucky Wild River), and all day hike or 4 hour shuttle tour to the Hensley Settlement (a restored Appalachian community that flourished in isolation years ago - guided tours - if your family has endurance of the all-day hiking or several hours of driving to get there).

LOST SQUADRON MUSEUM

1400 Dorchester Avenue, Middlesboro Airport, **Middlesboro** 40965

❑ Phone: (606) 248-1149. **Web: http://thelostsquadron.com/**
❑ Hours: Daily 8:00am-5:00pm
❑ Admission: FREE

The "Glacier Girl" is the plane to see here. It's a restored World War II P-38 fighter plane recovered in Greenland in 1992. The displays surrounding the plane tell stories about the landing and recovery and restoration in progress.

MOUNTAIN HOMEPLACE

(US 23 to SRKY 40 west to SR 2275 north, near Paintsville Lake)

Paintsville 41240

❑ Phone: (606) 297-1850 or (800) 542-5790 Tourism
    Web: www.mountainhomeplace.com
❑ Hours: Tuesday-Saturday 8:30am-5:00pm (April – October).
❑ Admission: $6.00 adult, $5.00 senior (55+), $4.00 child (6-17).
❑ Miscellaneous: Gift Shop and Crafts Store and an Auditorium. Before you tour, be sure to watch an informative introduction movie "The Land of Tomorrow" - narrated by the famous actor Richard Thomas whose ancestral roots are linked to the area. Many structures here are original.

Trained guides in period clothing demo skills and crafts - most activities are centuries old. The family farm area has giant oxen, goats, pigs, and chickens. The farm house was the center of family life and everything was self-contained. They grew crops and raised animals for food and crafted their housewares. The Church was the center of early pioneer settlements and the hard-working families took time out each month to gather and share and nurture one another. In the one-room schoolhouse you better behave so you don't get the "board of education". The blacksmith shop has "horse-tails" to tell. Did you know there were no outhouses and no toilet paper around in those days? Pick you favorite tree, mark it and find a nice big leaf! You'll soon discover these simple, harsh lives were only happy through worship and music. Impromptu concerts on the porch are easy to spot - just listen to the "pickers and grinners" playing music from the hills.

PAINTSVILLE LAKE STATE PARK

PO Box 726 (US 460 off KY 40), **Paintsville** 41240

❑   Phone: (606) 297-5253

Web: www.state.ky.us/agencies/parks/paintsv.htm

Lots of water for boating, skiing and fishing at yet another state park with abundant water areas. Along the 1140 acres of lake are wooded coves and steep cliffs that provide the background scenery for pristine water activities. There's a full service marina with rental houseboats, pontoons and fishing boats too.

PINE MOUNTAIN STATE RESORT PARK

1050 State Park Road (off US 25E)

Pineville 40977

❑   Phone: (606) 337-3066 or (800) 325-1712

Web: www.state.ky.us/agencies/parks/pinemtn2.htm

With 27 miles of trails leading through the valleys of the Kentucky Ridge State Forest. The trails are so popular, they have been given names like Hemlock Garden, Little Shepherd, Honeymoon Falls, Living Stairway and Rock Hotel. Chained Rock is a huge chain anchored to a boulder that seems to hold it in place. The new Pine Mountain Trail passes through the park. The resort lodge is on a mountaintop and cottages are available too. In a natural cove in the forest lies the Laurel Cove Amphitheater open for entertainment and festivals. There's also a campground, pool and mini-golf.

JENNY WILEY STATE RESORT PARK

75 Theatre Court (US 23/460 exit SR 3 east)
Prestonsburg 41653

❑   Phone: (606) 886-2711 or (800) 325-0142 reservations
     Web: www.jennywiley.com
❑   Hours: Open dawn to dusk.
❑   Admission: Free
❑   Miscellaneous: Lodge with dining room, Cottages, Campground,
     Gift Shop, Marina with boat launch and rentals, Pool, 10.25 miles
     of Hiking Trails, Picnicking.

Ride the Mountain Parkway Skylift on Sugar Camp Mountain 4700 ft. to the top (daily Memorial Day weekend-Labor day, Weekends in the Spring & Fall). The Nature Center has local wildlife, native plants, animals and local history. Named for a brave pioneer woman, Jenny Wiley, who was taken captive by Indians in 1789.   Wiley endured the loss of her children and brother, yet escaped after eleven months of captivity. She then started a new family and raised them - living until 72 years old. Weave thru the trails along Dewey Lake as your family pretends to imagine what a pioneer heroine must have endured.

JENNY WILEY THEATRE

121 Theatre Court (US 23/460 exit SR 3 east -in Jenny Wiley State Resort Park), Prestonsburg 41653

❑   Phone: (606) 886-9274 or (877) CALL-JWT
     Web: www.jwtheatre.com
❑   Hours: Tuesday-Sunday, mid-June to mid-August.
❑   Admission: $10.00-$17.00.

Broadway musicals (Peter Pan) and the story of "The Legend of Jenny Wiley" (performed two dates each summer).

KENTUCKY OPRY

Performances at the Mountain Arts Center (off US 23 South)

Prestonsburg 41653

❑   Phone: (606) 886-2623 or (888) 622-2787
Web: www.macarts.com

Family entertainment with programs of country, bluegrass, pop and gospel year-round. Look for "Munroe" the goofy character that is trying to get into showbiz or look for performances by students called Junior Pros.

KENTUCKY MUSIC HALL OF FAME AND MUSEUM

2590 Richmond Road (I-75 exit 62, east on Hwy 25)

Renfro Valley 40473

❑   Phone: (606) 256-1000 or (877) 356-3263
Web: www.kentuckymusicmuseum.com
❑   Hours: Tuesday-Saturday 10:00am-6:00pm, Sunday 9:00am-
5:00pm. January & February hours mostly just afternoons.
❑   Admission: $6.00 adult, $5.50 senior, $4.50 child (under 12).

The Hall of Fame includes exhibit cases for artifacts, instruments and costumes of honored inductees. You'll see and hear hundreds of entertainers like…Patty Loveless, Loretta Lynn, Bill Monroe, Rosemary Clooney, Billy Ray Cyrus, Ricky Skaggs and the Judds. Also included in the Museum is an instrument room (visitors touch, hear and perform); a sound booth where you can actually sing and record; and a timeline of Kentucky Music from front porch jamboree to radio to major public event concerts.

RENFRO VALLEY ENTERTAINMENT CENTER

I-75 exit 62 (US 25)

Renfro Valley 40473

❑ Phone: (606) 256-2638 or (800) 765-7464
  Web: www.renfrovalley.com

❑ Hours: Afternoon and evening shows. Sunday "Renfro Valley Gatherin" at 8:30am. Barn Dance on Saturday nights at 7:00pm. Village open March-December.

❑ Admission: Varies with production. Best to get on their mailing list for program offerings.

❑ Miscellaneous: RV Park.

Country music, family comedy and headliner concerts and festivals. "Kentucky's Country Music Capital" has an average of 12 shows weekly, Country restaurants, and Brush Arbor Log Shopping Village.

EASTERN KENTUCKY UNIVERSITY

Lancaster Avenue (off KY 876)

Richmond 40475

❑ Phone: (859) 622-1000. **Web: www.eku.edu/visitors/**

MEADOWBROOK FARM PROGRAM - (859) 622-1310. Meadowbrook Road (off KY 52). Agricultural production, dairy cattle, beef cattle, sheep, swine and cropping operations. Welcome during normal business hours or tours by appointment.

ATHLETIC TICKET OFFICE - (859) 622-2122. Eastern Bypass. Over ten varieties of sports including Collegiate basketball and football.

GREENHOUSE - (859) 622-2228, Eastern Bypass. Foliage propagation and production, rose and carnation beds.

HUMMEL PLANETARIUM AND SPACE THEATER - (859) 622-1547, Kit Carson Drive, Eastern Bypass. The 13th largest planetarium in the US with space science gift shop. Admission around $3.00+/person. Family Shows Thursday and Friday @ 6:00pm, Saturday @ 2:00pm & 6:00pm. Public Programs

Thursday & Friday 7:30pm, Saturday 3:30 & 7:30pm. Planetarium equipment used to stimulate the night sky consists of a giant star ball with the capacity of projecting over 10,000 stars, multiple projections of five planets, a sun, the moon, etc. - all of these operating simultaneously with surround sound. You can also travel throughout space and see the planets from other planets besides earth. At the end of each program, see the Kentucky night sky as it will look that night - look for your favorite constellations.

FORT BOONESBOROUGH STATE PARK

4375 Boonesborough Road (I-75 exit 95, I-64 exit at Winchester)

Richmond 40475

❑   Phone: (859) 527-3131

      Web: www.state.ky.us/agencies/parks/ftboones.htm

❑   Hours: Daily 9:00am-5:30pm (April-October). Wednesday-Sunday 10:00am-4:00pm (rest of year). Closed Thanksgiving and Christmastime.

❑   Admission: $4.00-$6.00 (age 7+). November-March admission is minimal.

❑   Miscellaneous: Campground, Marina/Boat Launch, Pool, some Hiking Trails, Mini-Golf, Picnicking, and Sandy beach.

After several skirmishes with Indians and rough terrain, Daniel Boone and his men reached the Kentucky River on April 1, 1775 and began laying out Kentucky's 2nd settlement. For many years this was a fortress, stopping point and trade center. The fort they constructed has been reconstructed as a working fort complete with cabins, blockhouses and period furnishings. Resident artisans share pioneer experiences and demonstrate pioneer crafts like pottery, candle-making, weaving and cooking. Riverside trails pass native plants and unusual geological sites. Begin your visit watching a film showing the struggles of the fort - esp. withstanding a 9-day attack by Indians and Frenchmen later known as "The Great Siege". A wonderful compliment to this visit is watching "Daniel Boone -The Legend" in Fort Harrod, southwest of here. Why are the names Blackfish and Henderson also important here? Look for interesting artifacts like the Clock

Rotisserie, giant corn mill, walking spinning wheel or "Pop goes the Weasel". Note: After leaving Ft. Boonesborough (because of cramped space), Daniel and family moved to a new site just north (I-75 exit 104, off KY 418 east). They suffered many hardships here and several family members are buried at this site. The Kentucky River Museum has numerous displays of prehistoric fishing to locks (some working models) and dams. Steamboats and showboats passed along this River...its visitors and river rats are all explored in this new museum.

LOU-RON HORSE SHOW CENTER

1741 Lancaster Road

Richmond 40475

❑   Phone: (859) 624-0889
❑   Hours: Horse shows every Sunday at 2:00pm.

Horse shows with barrel racing, team penning, poles, boarding stables to visit, riding lessons and children's events.

RICHMOND CIVIL WAR DRIVING TOUR

345 Lancaster Avenue (Richmond Visitor Center)

Richmond 40475

❑   Phone: (859) 626-8474 or (800) 866-3705
❑   Admission: Small fee charged for brochure and tape available
     (for purchase) at the visitor's center.

Follow Confederate troops on a 2 hour driving tour of the battle route of August 1862. There are six tour stations established in the approximate order the battle took place. Begin at the Top of Big Hill and on to places like Mt. Zion Church (used as a Union Hospital) to the Madison County Courthouse. After the Confederate advance, they later marched in triumph into Lexington and then took Frankfort. This was the only time in the war that the capitol of a Union state fell to Southern forces.

RICHMOND RACEWAY

US 52 E (Off Old Irvine Road)

Richmond 40475

❑ Phone: (859) 625-9408

❑ Hours: Saturday night at 8:00pm (May-early October)

A 3/10th mile clay, oval track with several different classes of stock car racing.

WHITE HALL STATE HISTORIC SITE

500 White Hall Shrine Road (I-75 exit 95)

Richmond 40475

❑ Phone: (859) 623-9178

   Web: www.state.ky.us/agencies/parks/whthall.htm

❑ Hours: Daily 9:00am-5:30pm (April-October). Closed Mondays and Tuesdays (September & October).

❑ Admission: $4.50 adult, $2.50 children (6-12)

❑ Tours: Last tour begins one hour before closing. One hour long.

❑ Miscellaneous: Gift shop, picnicking.

The home of Cassius Marcellus Clay: emancipationist, newspaper publisher, Minister to Russia, and friend to Abraham Lincoln. Overall, he was quite a character and lived grandly (notice the larger than life doors). The restored 44 room Italianate mansion is about 200 years old and has period and heirloom furnishings, a working cookhouse, outside slave /servant quarters, and many unique features for its day. They had running water and central heating (look for the outlets hidden in fireplaces and behind little doors). How were orators (like Clay) similar to our superstars today?

BYBEE POTTERY

(US 52 east)

Richmond (Waco) 40385

❑ Phone: (859) 369-5350

❑ Hours: Monday-Friday 8:00am-Noon and 12:30-3:30pm. Kilns open Monday, Wednesday, and Friday at 8:00am.

For updates visit our website: www.kidslovepublications.com

❑   Admission: FREE
❑   Tours: Group tours are best scheduled on Tuesdays and
     Thursdays. Self-guided looking anytime.

The oldest pottery West of the Alleghenies (established before 1845) and still owned by the Cornelison Family. When you get there, you'll see it looks much the same as it did then. Dirt floors, warped wood walls and clay dust everywhere really add to the feeling. If you show up and take an impromptu tour, the potters will gladly answer questions while continuing their work. One potter told us the trick to centering your piece is "keeping your elbows down". We also asked about the secret to Bybee's success - Answer: Handmade individual pieces and low prices. We would agree. By the time we got there on a Wednesday morning (8:30am), every showroom shelf was empty and people were paying for their purchases. They have a ritual for shopping there - you have to witness it!

CARR CREEK STATE PARK

PO Box 249 (KY 15 south)

Sassafras 41759

❑   Phone: (606) 642-4050
     Web: www.state.ky.us/agencies/parks/carrcrk.htm

Camping and the beach are surrounded by mountains and sun. There's also a full-service marina, boating, fishing and rental boats too.

KENTUCKY REPTILE ZOO

200 L & E Railroad (1 mile south of Mountain Pkwy, exit 33 off SR KY 11)

Slade 40376

❑   Phone: (606) 663-9160
     Web: www.geocities.com/kentuckyreptilezoo
❑   Hours: Daily 11:00am-6:00pm (Memorial Day-Labor Day).
     Friday-Sunday only 11:00am-6:00pm (March-May, September-November).
❑   Admission: $5.00 adult, $3.00 child (4-15).

Kentucky Reptile Zoo (cont.)

The zoo is also a captive born venom lab with extractions and live reptile presentations held daily on the hour from 1:00-5:00pm. The live reptile exhibits include more than 75 species of lizards, turtles, alligators and snakes. The zoo is now breeding successfully to hopefully use the extracted substances to produce medical and research projects. Look for the vide variety of cobras, rattlesnakes and vipers too.

NATURAL BRIDGE STATE RESORT PARK

2135 Natural Bridge Road (I-64 exit on to the Mountain Parkway southeast to KY 11)

Slade 40376

- ❑   Phone: (606) 663-2214 or (800) 325-1710 reservations
  Web: www.state.ky.us/agencies/parks/natbridg.htm
- ❑   Hours: Dawn to Dusk
- ❑   Admission: FREE
- ❑   Miscellaneous: Lodge with dining, Cottages, Campground, Gift Shop, Pool, Mini-golf, Picnicking, Weekly Square Dances at Hoe Down Islands, Nature Preserve, Mill Creek Lake, Balanced Rock, Devil's Gulch, salt peter mines, a cave. Trails End Horse Camp - guided horse tours, primitive camping adventures (SR 3330, (606) 464-9530). Red River Gorge Geological Area is spectacular in its own right!

All we can really say is WOW! Even though we researched this place for hours before coming to visit - it truly was amazing to hike or chair lift up to the bridge. A natural sandstone arch, the bridge spans 78 feet long and 65 feet high. There are no guardrails (keep a strong hold of children up there...please) and we were one-third of the way across the Bridge before we realized we were walking on top of it! The hikes to scenic overlooks and narrow paths (Fat Man's Misery) were shorter than most, making it very accessible for families. One trail walks you right under the bridge too! May we suggest you try a one-way or round-trip ride on the Natural Bridge Skylift. The Skylift takes you slowly and gradually through some of the most beautiful scenery in the Appalachian area. Sloped gently at first, then a sharp, steep climb up the final stretch - it will leave you mighty anxious to conquer a short trail (600 feet) to the bridge. One way trips are $3.00 (ages 4+) and round-trips are $5.00 for adults and $4.00 for children (4-12). Open Easter weekend thru the end of October at 10:00 am daily. Closing times are posted daily. The whole experience is like a giant amusement park adventure ride!

VAN LEAR HISTORICAL SOCIETY COAL CAMP MUSEUM

Miller Circle (SRKY 321 to SRKY 302, 6 miles southeast of downtown)

Van Lear 41265

❏ Phone: (606) 789-9725

Web: www.geocities.com/Heartland/Ranch/7827/

❏ Hours: Monday-Saturday 9:00am-3:00pm (March-November 15)

This former Consolidated Coal Company office building has a model of the 1920's & 1930's company town, an original doctor's office, and a post office. Old carbide lamps, breast augers, and other such items are featured. Stop at the General Store down the road to ask Herman Webb (Loretta's brother) for a tour of the real Butcher Hollow homestead.

APPALSHOP

91 Madison Avenue (Hwy 15 bypass to downtown, just past the curve and bridge)

Whitesburg 41858

❏ Phone: (606) 633-0108. **Web: www.appalshop.org**
❏ Admission: FREE
❏ Tours: Guided tours are available by reservation, Monday-Friday 9:00am-5:00pm, closed holidays.

This center focuses on Appalachian culture. They produce a variety of films, videotapes and musical recordings. The highlight for children, on tour, is the stop in the non-commercial community radio station. In the on-hour room the kids can talk on the radio! There is also a visual art exhibit in the gallery for viewing and, depending on the schedule, there may be something going on in the theater or a festival in progress. Stop by on your way out to buy some old-fashioned candy or just listen in on the locals at the Caudill General Store & History Center.

KENTUCKY SPLASH WATER PARK

1050 Hwy 92 West (I-75 exit 11)

Williamsburg 40769

❑ Phone: (606) 549-6065. **Web: www.kentuckysplash.com**

❑ Hours: Daily, except Sundays 11:00am-7:00pm (Memorial Day weekend thru mid-August). Sundays 12:30-6:30pm. Extended hours for indoor activities.

❑ Admission: $13.00-$15.00 (age 3+). Land Lovers $3.00. Half price admission after 3:00pm.

The Hal Rogers Family Entertainment Center is home to the Kentucky Splash Water Park. The park includes an 18,000 square ft. wave pool, a drift river, a kiddy activity pool, a triple slide complex, a go-kart track, a championship miniature golf course, an arcade, a batting cage and even a café and gift shop. Changing rooms/lockers are available.

Chapter 5
Area - West (W)

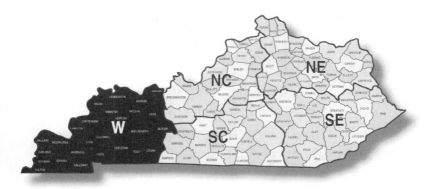

Our Favorites...

* Pratt Memorial Museum - Ft. Campbell

* Land Between the Lakes - Golden Pond

* Trail of Tears - Hopkinsville Area

* State Park Resorts on Lake Barkley & Kentucky Lake

* International Bluegrass Museum - Owensboro

* River Heritage Museum - Paducah

" State Park Trailriding Fun "

LAKE BARKLEY STATE RESORT PARK

Box 790 (US 68W to KY 1489)

Cadiz 42211

❑ Phone: (800) 325-1708, (270) 924-1131 Lodge, (800) 295-1878 Marina. **www.kystateparks.com/agencies/parks/lakebark.htm**

❑ Miscellaneous: Eagles Weekend late February. Offering eagle viewing trips and live animal evening programs. Admission.

The world-class lodge of post-and-beam wood construction with lots of windows for viewing is what most think of when mentioning Barkley. A spacious campground, lighted airstrip and Fitness Center with indoor/outdoor pools are favorites too. The Barkley Dam is where to watch barges going through a large lock off KY 453 near Grand Rivers and stop in the center for audiovisual exhibits relating to the steamboat era. For private accommodations, enjoy one of the nine two-bedroom, two-bath cottages with lake or wooded views. For rustic charm, Lake Barkley offers 4 two-bedroom log cabins. Each have unique appeal, and offer screened-in porches or decks. Tableware, cooking utensils and fresh linens are provided. Also on the premises are a marina, camping, boat rentals, horseback riding, tennis and recreation programs.

KENTUCKY LAKE MOTOR SPEEDWAY

950 Truck Plaza (I-24 exit 27 to the Interstate Frontage Road)

Calvert City 42029

❑ Phone: (270) 395-3600. **Web: www.klms.com**

Dirt track racing, monster trucks, truck/tractor pulls, rodeos and occasional concerts. Many NASCAR races including late models, open wheel modified and limited sportsmen plus sprint.

COLUMBUS-BELMONT STATE PARK

350 Park Road (36 miles southwest of Paducah on KY 80 & KY 58)

Columbus 42032

❑ Phone: (270) 677-2327

Web: www.state.ky.us/agencies/parks/columbus.htm

❑ Hours: 9:00am-5:00pm daily (May-September). Weekends only (April & October).

❑ Admission: Park is FREE. Museum is $1.50-$2.00 per person.

❑ Miscellaneous: Campground, Gift shop, Boat launches and marina, hiking trails, mini-golf, picnicking.

Recall the 1861 Battle of Belmont and the fight to control this important waterway called the "Gibraltar of the West". But a General named Grant outflanked the "Gibraltar" and forced its evacuation. See the massive chain and anchor used by the South to block passage of the Union gunboats and the earthen trenches dug to protect almost 20,000 Confederate troops. The museum was once a Civil War hospital but now serves as a display of Indian artifacts and Civil War relics. A video is shown.

PENNYRILE FOREST STATE RESORT PARK

20781 Pennyrile Lodge Road
(KY 109N, 20 miles NW of Hopkinsville)

Dawson Springs 42408

❑ Phone: (270) 797-3421 lodge or (800) 325-1711 reservations

Web: www.state.ky.us/agencies/parks/pennyril.htm

Named for the Pennyroyal plant found in the surrounding woodlands, the place is good for a rustic get-a-way by lodge or cottage. The rustic wood and stone lodge, with 24 rooms, sits serenely on a high cliff overlooking Pennyrile Lake. The park has 13 cottages located in the wooded lodge area and on the shores of Pennyrile Lake. The one and two-bedroom cottages have unique features, offering wooded or lake views, and such amenities as private boat and fishing docks, fireplaces, or screened-in porches. Tableware, cooking utensils, and fresh linens are provided. Also available are mountain biking trails, campground, gift shop, boat rentals, hiking trials, tennis, mini-golf, and recreation programs.

KENTUCKY OPRY

❑   88 Chilton Lane (Jackson Purchase/Carroll Pkwy exit 47)

Draffenville 42025

❑   Phone: (270)- 527-3869

Web: www.kentuckylake.com/kentuckyopry

❑   Hours: Shows Every Friday night during the months of June, July, August & December. Shows Every Saturday Night Year Round. Central Time.

❑   Admission: ~$11.00 adults, ~Half-price children

This show presents some of the finest talent in Kentucky. It's wholesome entertainment for the entire family - featuring country, gospel, down-home comedy and Bluegrass music.

DOGWOOD LAKES RESORT & FUNPARK

7777 State Route 973 (2 miles from Lake Malone, US 431S)

Dunmor 42339

❑   Phone: (270) 657-8380. **Web: www.dogwoodlakes.com**

❑   Hours: Daily basically 11:00am-5:00pm (Memorial Day weekend thru first full week of August). Extended weekend hours. Also open most long weekends (Special events, May- mid-September).

❑   Admission: Gate & Swimming: $4.00-$5.00 (age 3+). Slides additional fee ($6.50 - $12.00 armbands) .

❑   Miscellaneous: Many special events like Country Jam (June), Gospel Day (August). Concession stand and gift shop. Activities for kids on weekends.

Relax and enjoy the beach on one of three clear lakes. Play and splash on the swimming decks, paddle boats, kiddie play area or waterslides. Full hook-up camp sites and Top Dog Camping Sheds are available for overnights.

LAKE MALONE STATE PARK

PO Box 93 (from Greenville, take US 431 south to KY 973)

Dunmor 42339

❑   Phone: (270) 657-2111

    Web: www.state.ky.us/agencies/parks/lmalone.htm

❑   This small park is enclosed by a wonderful 200-foot sandstone bluff and hardwood forest. The park has a campground, marina, beach, rental boats and hiking trails. The mile and one-half Laurel Trail is an easy-rated hiking trail providing picturesque views of many rock walls, once used as shelters by prehistoric Native Americans.

VENTURE RIVER WATER PARK

280 Park Place (I-24 exit 40, US 62)

Eddyville 42038

❑   Phone: (270) 388-7999. **Web: www.ventureriver.com**

❑   Hours: Daily 10:00am-7:00pm (Summer). Central Time

❑   Admission: $14.00-$17.00 average general admission (age 3+). Seniors & After 4:00pm are about half of the price.

With kiddie rides added to five body slides, two tube slides, a Wave Pool, cyclone, kiddie pool, Frog Island, action river, and beach volleyball - there's plenty of summertime fun. Waloopas twin enclosed water slides are the newest feature.

MINERAL MOUND STATE PARK

(off US62/641, KY 93 south of Eddyville, north of the I-24 exit)

Eddyville 42044

❑   Phone: (270) 362-4271 Kentucky Dam

    Web: www.state.ky.us/agencies/parks/mineral.htm

On the shores of Lake Barkley, this park is historically linked to the author F. Scott Fitzgerald - this was once the farm of Fitzgerald's wife's grandfather. Boat launch, some hiking trails.

JEFFERSON DAVIS MONUMENT STATE HISTORIC SITE

PO Box 157 (US 68 east), **Fairview** 42221

❑   Phone: (270) 886-1765

   Web: www.state.ky.us/agencies/parks/jefdav2.htm

❑   Hours: Daily 9:00am-5:00pm (May-October).

❑   Admission: $2.00 elevator.

The name Jefferson Davis is best known as the man elected President of the Confederate States of America in 1861 preceding the Civil War. Ironically, both Davis and Abraham Lincoln were born in Kentucky in log cabins within one year and 100 miles apart. A 351 obelisk marks the birthplace of Jefferson Davis, born here on June 3, 1808. The monument features an elevator to the top of the structure for a panoramic view of the surrounding countryside. The visitor center enlightens visitors on the unique history that caused its preservation. A short DVD presentation and exhibits detail the political life of Davis before and after the Civil War and the building of the monument. Also told is the little known story of the Kentucky "Orphan Brigade." The center includes a gift shop featuring Kentucky handcrafts, souvenirs, books and Civil War memorabilia.

PRATT MEMORIAL MUSEUM, DON F.

Bldg. 5702, Tennessee Ave. (Ft. Campbell, US 41A, Gate 4 entrance), **Fort Campbell** 42241

❑   Phone: (270) 798-3215 or (270) 798-4986

   www.campbell.army.mil/pratt or www.fortcampbell.com

❑   Hours: Daily 9:30am-4:30pm. Closed Christmas and New Years. Central Time

❑   Admission: FREE

❑   Miscellaneous: Ft. Campbell is home to the 101st Airborne Division (known as the "Screaming Eagles"), the 5th Special Forces Group and the 160th Special Operations Aviation Regiment.

Pratt Memorial Museum (cont.)

Probably the best thing to check out are the WW II cargo gliders displayed on this large military reservation museum. Exhibits on the history of Ft. Campbell and the many units stationed here from the present back to World War II include: uniforms, photos, restored aircraft and some weapons. There's even a display with Adolph Hitler's walking stick. The new, <u>WINGS OF LIBERTY MILITARY MUSEUM</u> will open to positively replace the current structure. It will be located directly off US 41A. The approximately 80,000 square feet facility includes a 200-seat IMAX-style theater, art gallery, cafe, book store/gift shop, and an artifact storage area. The main exhibit area will display artifacts ranging from the WWII D-Day invasion of Normandy to Operation Desert Shield/Desert Storm in Kuwait and Iraq and operations in Panama, Somalia, Haiti, and Bosnia.

KENTUCKY DAM VILLAGE

PO Box 69 (I-24 east to exit 27, US 62 to US 641east)

Gilbertsville 42044

❑   Phone: (270) 362-4271 Lodge, (800) 325-0146 reservations, (270) 362-8386 Marina.
    Web: www.state.ky.us/agencies/parks/kydam2.htm
❑   Miscellaneous: Gathering of Eagles Weekend in mid-January. Viewing and learning eagle spotting techniques and finding their habitats. Admission.

This is one of three resort parks surrounding Land Between the Lakes National Recreation Area. With an abundance of water, the most popular sports are boating, water-skiing, snorkeling and fishing. The main lodge has private balconies or patios and fine dining. With 68 cottages, Kentucky Dam Village has more choices for overnight accommodations than any other state park. You can choose a one, two, or three-bedroom cottage with one or two baths. Tableware, cooking utensils, and fresh linens are provided. There's also a campground, gift shop, airport, marina, boat rentals, pool, beach, tennis, mini-golf and recreation programs.

For updates visit our website: www.kidslovepublications.com

MAGGIE'S JUNGLE GOLF

7301 US Hwy 641 N (near Kentucky Dam), **Gilbertsville** 42044

❑   Phone: (270) 362-8933

❑   Hours: Call for seasonal hours and admission pricing.

Putt-putt at its best. Enjoy a combination of shuffleboard, putt-putt and live animals with a petting zoo, nature trail, covered bridges and a picnic area or take a ride in the Safari Car. The nature trail has pygmy goats, llamas, pot-bellied pigs, camel, and miniature horses.

LAND BETWEEN THE LAKES NATIONAL RECREATION AREA

100 Van Morgan Drive (I-24w exit 31, SRKY 453 south to the Trace on US 68/KY80 between Kentucky Lake and Lake Barkley)

Golden Pond 42211

❑   Phone: (270) 924-2020. **Web: www.lbl.org**

❑   Hours: Open year-round but some facilities are closed during winter. See specific facility hours below. Central Time.

❑   Admission: FREE, except specific facilities listed below.

❑   Miscellaneous: Kentucky Kayak Kountry Phone: 270-362-0081.

"Land Between the Lakes" located between:

❑   **KENTUCKY LAKE** - a top fishing , water sport and water recreation area on the largest lake in Kentucky. Over 2300 miles of shoreline with the Kentucky Dam (US 62/641) at Gilbertsville across the Tenn. River is 208 ft. high and 8400 ft. wide.

❑   **LAKE BARKLEY** – 2nd largest Kentucky lake with 1000 miles of shoreline for recreation and the lake for fishing. The Barclay Dam is off KY 453 near Grand Rivers across the Cumberland River.

Facilities available:

❑   **GOLDEN POND VISITORS CENTER** - centrally located, has info, displays, a planetarium and video orientation. Open 9:00am-5:00pm, year-round, except Thanksgiving, Christmas and New Year's. Planetarium admission is between $2.00-$3.00.

Land Between The Lakes (cont.)

❑ **ELK & BISON PRAIRIE** - 1 mile north on the Trace. 750 acre preserve is a recreation of the prairie that existed over 200 years ago - mostly grassland and American Indian era animals like bison, elk, deer, wild turkeys, coyotes, rabbits, hawks, owls and songbirds. A drive-thru park with interpretive displays at various spots. Daily dawn-dusk. Admission $3.00 per vehicle.

❑ **THE HOMEPLACE** - 15 miles south on the Trace (actually in Tennessee, just over the border). A living-history farm which re-creates the farming and daily activities of a typical rural family living between the Cumberland and Tennessee rivers in the 1850s. Interpreters are dressed in period clothing and talk to guests while doing daily chores. There are 16 buildings (some original), an interpretive center with exhibits and video orientation, and many seasonal festivals most every weekend. Monday-Saturday 9:00am-5:00pm, Sunday 10:00am-5:00pm (April-October); Closed Mondays and Tuesdays in March and November. Admission $3.50 adults, $2.00 children (5-12).

❑ **THE NATURE STATION** - north on the Trace, then east on Mulberry Flat Road, follow signs. An environmental education center offering canoe rentals, trails and live animal exhibits. Special weekend events March thru November. Bald eagle viewing excursions by boat and van in the winter months. Open Monday-Saturday 9am-5pm, Sunday 10am-5pm (April-October); Closed Mondays and Tuesdays in March and November. Area is FREE but Nature Station is $3.50 adults, $2.00 children (5-12).

PATTI'S 1880'S SETTLEMENT

1793 J.H. O'Bryan Drive (I-24 exit 31 south)

Grand Rivers 42045

❑ Phone: (270) 362-8844 or (888) 736-2515
   Web: www.pattis-settlement.com

❑ Hours: Open daily 10:30am-8:00pm. Central time. Moderate prices. Children's menu.

Relaxed dining in 1880s atmosphere featuring homemade pies, flower pot bread and 2" thick pork chops. Historic log cabin settlement with unique shops, miniature golf and animal park. Try the mile-high lemon meringue pie, Bill's Boatsinker or Sawdust pie.

ROBERT PENN WARREN BIRTHPLACE MUSEUM

Corner of Third and Cherry Streets

Guthrie 42234

❑   Phone: (270) 483-2683

    Web: www.robertpennwarren.com/birthpla.htm

❑   Hours: Tuesday-Saturday 11:30am-3:30pm, Sunday 2:00-4:00pm. Closed holidays. Central time.

❑   Admission: Donations

Here is the boyhood home of America's first poet laureate, Robert Penn Warren, author of 10 novels and 16 volumes of poetry. Warren lived here in the early 1900's until age 16. Warren is best known for his fiction novel " All the King's Men" (Pulitzer 1946). Inspire your children by viewing photos, books and works of the author on display.

HARDIN SOUTHERN RAILROAD

(Purchase Pkwy. Exit US 641, left on SR 402)

Hardin 42048

❑   Phone: (270) 437-4555. **Web: www.hsrr.com**

❑   Admission: $11.00 adult, $6.50 child (3-12).

❑   Tours: Saturday twice in the afternoon and Sunday departure around 2:00pm (Memorial Day - end of October). Central Time. Seasonal theme rides too (see seasonal chapter).

An 18-mile nostalgic excursion through the beautiful Clarks River Valley on a 100+ year old railroad. Sit in reclining seats with climate controlled coaches while watching for forest and farmland along your 2 hour journey.

KENLAKE STATE RESORT PARK

542 Kenlake Road (I-24 north, exit US 68/KY 80W OR I-24 to
Purchase Pkwy, then US 68E)

Hardin 42048

❑ Phone: (800) 325-0143 reservations, Lodge (270) 474-2211.
Marina (270) 474-2245
Web: www.state.ky.us/agencies/parks/kenlake2.htm
❑ Miscellaneous: Eagle weekend early February. View bald eagle
in natural habitat. Evening programs and refreshments.
Admission.

Located on the western shore of Kentucky Lake, this park features
an indoor tennis center and pro shop, 200 miles of woodland trails
and a grand hotel. For more private accommodations, you may
choose a one, two, or three-bedroom cottage with one or two baths.
These cottages offer beautiful lake, wooded, or golf course views
with features that include decks and screened-in porches.
Tableware, cooking utensils, and linens are provided. Also
campgrounds, marina, boat rentals, a pool, horseback riding trails
and recreation programs.

OHIO COUNTY MUSEUM COMPLEX

Main Street

Hartford 42347

❑ Phone: (270) 298-3749
❑ Hours: Monday-Friday 9:00am-4:00pm (April-October).
Central Time.
❑ Admission: $2.00

Different structures like a country store, 1838 log cabin, one-room
school house, a restored L&N caboose and another building called
Rusty Relics are all here together to explore county history.

HANCOCK COUNTY MUSEUM

Depot Street (River & Depot Streets)

Hawesville 42348

❑   Phone: (270) 314-5688

❑   Hours: Sunday 2:00-4:00pm (April-October). Central Time.

❑   Admission: Donations.

The building that the museum is housed in is an early 1900's wooden L&N depot which helps give you the feeling of going back to the time of turn-of-the-century family life and riverboat life. There's even an 1867 courtroom inside.

JOHN JAMES AUDUBON STATE PARK

3100 US Hwy 41N (US 41 north, near Ohio River)

Henderson 42420

❑   Phone: (270) 826-2247 or (270) 827-1893 Center
     Web: www.state.ky.us/agencies/parks/audubon2.htm

❑   Hours: Park open dawn to dusk. Center open 10:00am-5:00pm
     daily except Winter holidays. Central Time.

❑   Admission: $2.50-4.00 for Center.

Named for the first naturalist to artistically portray and protect birds - this is where he observed the subjects of his paintings from 1810-1819.   Part of the Mississippi Flyway of migration, the Museum & Center seek to interpret Audubon's life through his original art, personal memorabilia, bird observation areas and the Discovery area with hands-on exhibits and educational themed programs.   Be sure to look for a lovely souvenir reprint of his works - most notably the great horned owl and woodpecker series. Also found on site are campgrounds, small rental cottages, rental boats, hiking trails, golf and mini-golf, tennis and lots of birding and fishing.

TRAIL OF TEARS COMMEMORATIVE PARK

US 41 South, Pembroke Road

Hopkinsville 42240

❑   Phone: (270) 886-8033. **Web: www.trailoftears.org**

❑   Hours: Park open during daylight hours, daily. Heritage Center: Thursday-Saturday 10:00am-2:00pm.

This historic park is one of the few documented sites of actual trail and campsites used during the forced removal of the Cherokee people to "Indian Territory". It was used as an encampment in 1838 and 1839. The Park is situated on a portion of the campground used by the Cherokees on the infamous Trail of Tears and includes the gravesites of Chiefs White Path and Fly Smith. The park includes a Heritage Center, picnic areas and ample parking.

HOPKINS COUNTY HISTORICAL MUSEUM & GOVERNOR RUBY LAFFOON'S BIRTHPLACE

107 Union Street

Madisonville 42431

❑   Phone: (270) 821-3986

❑   Hours: Monday-Friday 1:00-5:00pm, closed holidays. Central Time.

❑   Admission: $1.00 (12 and older).

The restored log cabin is furnished as it was when the former governor lived there in the late 1800s. The museum displays old photos, civil War items and other 1800-1900 coal-mining memorabilia.

CLEMENT MINERAL MUSEUM

205 North Walker Street

Marion 42064

❑   Phone: (270) 965-4263

Web: www.clementmineralmuseum.com

For updates visit our website: www.kidslovepublications.com

❑   Hours: Tuesday-Saturday 9:00am-3:00pm. Central time
❑   Admission: $3.00

This is the area where 19th century pirates once robbed flatboats along the river. In the museum are more than 30,000 native mineral specimens shown in 5 different exhibit areas. The fluorite crystals with a blacklight show is a must see.

CAMP BRECKINRIDGE MUSEUM
1116 North Village Road (US 60)
Morganfield 42437

❑   Phone: (270) 389-4420. **Web: www.breckinridge-arts.org**
❑   Hours: Tuesday-Friday 10:00am-3:00pm, Saturday 10:00am-4:00pm, Sunday 1:00-5:00pm
❑   Admission: $3.00 adult, $1.00 student

Located in the old officer's club that was purchased and renovated by the county, the interior still contains over 40 "European scene" murals painted on the wall by German POW Daniel Mayer. This site was a training facility for soldiers and a POW prison during WW II. Also, see local history and art displays.

PLAYHOUSE IN THE PARK
Gil Hopson Drive, **Murray** 42071

❑   Phone: (270) 759-1752
❑   Hours: Year-round productions are performed Thursday-Saturday evenings and Sunday matinees. Central time.

Family entertainment of comedies, musicals (like Heidi), dramas and mysteries. Box of Frogs Childrens Theatre.

BEN HAWES STATE PARK
400 Boothfield Road (4 miles west of Owensboro off US 60)
Owensboro 42301

❑   Phone: (270) 684-9808
     Web: www.state.ky.us/agencies/parks/benhawes.htm

Known mostly for its golf course, there's also hiking trails and an archery range.

OWENSBORO MUSEUM OF SCIENCE AND HISTORY

220 Daviess Street (off US 60)

Owensboro 42302

❑ Phone: (270) 687-2732
❑ Hours: Monday-Saturday 10:00am-5:00pm, Sunday 1:00-5:00pm. Central time.
❑ Admission: $3.00 general, $10.00 family.

The science aspect focuses on disciplines like astronomy, geology and botany. Cultural aspects of archeology, county history and Native Americans are explored too. Of special interest to children is the live reptile collection, the Government Education Center featuring exhibits that explain how government works, and a children's hands-on exhibit.

INTERNATIONAL BLUEGRASS MUSIC MUSEUM

117 Daviess Street (RiverPark Center)

Owensboro 42303

❑ Phone: (270) 926-7891. **Web: www.bluegrass-museum.org**
❑ Hours: Tuesday-Friday 10:00am-5:00pm, Saturday & Sunday 1:00-5:00pm.
❑ Admission: $5.00 adult, $2.00 student (age 7-16).

Visit the Bluegrass Hall of Honor, a heritage theatre and new interactive exhibits. View a showcase of historically significant bluegrass instruments, meet the varieties of cultures evolving the roots of bluegrass, or listen to a bluegrass jukebox. Create your own bluegrass mix in the studio or stand under "listening domes" situated throughout the concourse.

CIVIL WAR MUSEUM, TILGHMAN

631 Kentucky Avenue (7th Street & Kentucky)

Paducah 42001

❑   Phone: (270) 575-1870

❑   Hours: Wednesday-Saturday Noon-4:00pm.Central time.

❑   Admission: $1.50 general (age 12+).

Restored home of General Lloyd Tilghman includes Civil War exhibits that explain Paducah's role in the war.

MARKET HOUSE THEATRE

141 Kentucky Avenue (Market House Square)

Paducah 42001

❑   Phone: (270) 444-6828 or (888) MHT-PLAY

Web: www.mhtplay.com

15-20 productions per season of comedy, musicals and children's shows like The Velveteen Rabbit or Annie Jr. and the Children's Choir.

NATIONAL QUILT MUSEUM

215 Jefferson Street (I-24 Downtown Loop)

Paducah 42001

❑   Phone: (270) 442-8856. **Web: www.quiltmuseum.org**

❑   Hours: Monday-Saturday 10:00am-5:00pm year round. Sunday 1:00-5:00pm (April-October). Closed all Winter and Spring holidays. Central Time.

❑   Admission: $5.00 adult, $3.00 student (age 12+).

❑   Miscellaneous: Gift shop and bookstore.

Changing theme exhibits display over 200 quilts from old-fashioned to modern to colorful to unique or abstract. The building has eight stained glass windows with designs based on quilt patterns.

PADUCAH INTERNATIONAL RACEWAY
4445 Shemwell Lane
Paducah 42001

❑   Phone: (270) 898-7469.   Web: www.racingcorner.com/pir/
❑   Hours: Some Friday and most every Saturday night beginning at
     7:00pm, gates open at 4:00pm (May-October) Central time.

A 3/8 mile, high bank dirt track. Racing, late model, modified, pre-stock and street stock autos.

RIVER HERITAGE MUSEUM & FLOODWALL MURALS
117 S. Water Street (RiverPlace)
Paducah 42001

❑   Phone: (270) 575-9958
❑   Hours: Monday-Saturday 9:30am-5:00pm, Sunday 1:00-5:00pm.
❑   Admission: $5.00 adult, $3.00 child (3-12).
❑   Tours: By reservation

Overlooking the confluence of the Tennessee and Ohio Rivers stands the Center for Maritime Education. View river navigation simulation in progress from an observation deck. Permanent and changing exhibits tell the story of the Four Rivers Region, a geographic area that encompasses the Ohio, Cumberland, Tennessee and Mississippi Rivers. The museum features water-filled exhibits including a working lock and dam model. A build-a-river exhibit allows the visitor to maneuver sand and water to form various river configurations. A dredging exhibit shows how the sediment of river bottoms is moved in order to improve navigational channels. This exhibit also features various samples of mussel species. Mud microscopes enable the visitor to view the river bottoms. Across the street, Western Kentucky's rich heritage comes alive on **FLOODWALL MURALS** (800-Paducah) painted by Muralist, Robert Dafford. The floodwalls have vivid scenes painted from history include the Standing Watch View From the Pilot House, the Christening of the Eleanor, and the Visit of the Three "Queens" to Paducah. (The American Queen, the Delta

Queen and the Mississippi Queen.) Bronze interpretive panels explain the content and enable onlookers to understand the content of each mural.

WHITEHAVEN WELCOME CENTER
Kentucky Welcome Center (I-24E exit 7, US 45)

Paducah 42001

❑ Phone: (270) 554-2077 or (800) 225-TRIP
   Web: www.paducah-tourism.org
❑ Hours: Daily 8:00am-6:00pm. Central time.
❑ Admission: FREE
❑ Tours: Daily on the half hour 1:00-4:00pm
❑ Miscellaneous: Modern restroom facilities open 24 hours.

Whitehaven mansion was built in the mid-1800s and the historical tourist center is designed to offer a glimpse of the state's past and symbolize Kentucky's position as a gateway to the South. Exhibits highlight Paducah native, Alben Barkley, Senator and US Vice-President.

WILLIAM CLARK MARKET HOUSE MUSEUM
121 South Second Street (Center of the Market House Square)

Paducah 42001

❑ Phone: (270) 443-7759
❑ Hours: Monday-Saturday Noon-4:00pm. Closed in January & February and major holidays. Central Time.
❑ Admission: $1.00-$2.00 (age 6+).

Articles displayed from Paducah's history in the 1905 Market House. Find inside an 1870's drug store, Civil War relics, river and local history exhibits.

YEISER ART CENTER

200 Broadway Street

Paducah 42001

❑ Phone: (270) 442-2453. **Web: www.yeiserartcenter.com**

❑ Hours: Tuesday-Saturday 10:00am-4:00pm Closed major holidays. Central time.

Changing exhibitions of Kentucky and national artists, contemporary and historical art forms, painting, photography, sculpture, prints, mixed media, fibers. National Fibers Exhibit each spring. Call ahead for the Elements in Art handout that helps your children understand the basics of art in every work they view. The art appreciation card can be utilized with any exhibit that they sponsor. The card can be used by the child alone or with an adult. It provides information based on the elements of art, poses questions, and suggests that the child interact (visually) with the works. They also have interactive panels that are hands on. They show an example of a recognized work of art and then invite the children to draw, paint, touch, or move items to illustrate the various concepts shown on the panels.

ADSMORE HOUSE MUSEUM

304 North Jefferson Street

Princeton 42445

❑ Phone: (270) 365-3114

❑ Hours: Tuesday-Saturday 11:00am-4:00pm, Sunday 1:00-4:00pm. Central time.

❑ Admission: $5.00 adult, $4.50 senior (65+), $2.00 child (2-12).

A c. 1857 Greek Revival home restored to late Victorian. Period-costumed guides give the feeling of that place and time. The Gunshop is restored to 1844 to tell the story of Princeton's first gunsmith. Scenes portray a funeral, a wedding, the Night Riders 1906 raid, or Christmas 1901.

WICKLIFFE MOUNDS

94 Green Street (northwest on US 51 / 60 / 62)

Wickliffe 42087

❑ Phone: (270) 335-3681

Web: **http://campus.murraystate.edu/org/wmrc/wmrc.htm**

❑ Hours: Daily 9:00am-4:30pm (March-November). Central Time.

❑ Admission: $5.00 adult, $4.75 senior (55+), $4.00 child (6-11).

This Research Center and Archeological Site is where they've excavated prehistoric (1100-1350AD) Mississippian Mound culture villages. Unearthed for current viewing is a burial mound, home sites and temple mounds with different interpretive exhibits that illustrate prehistoric Indian life and also explain how the archeologists do their work.

Chapter 6

Seasonal & Special Events

JANUARY

NATIVE AMERICAN WEEKEND

SC - Jamestown, Lake Cumberland SRP. (800) 325-1709. Demos of Native American culture including a buffalo meat dinner. (Last weekend in January).

FEBRUARY

LINCOLN'S BIRTHDAY CELEBRATION

NC - Hodgenville, Abraham Lincoln Birthplace NHS. (270) 358-3137. The president is honored by a procession to the symbolic birthplace cabin and the placement of a wreath on the door. (on Lincoln's Birthday)

EDISON BIRTHDAY PARTY

NC - Louisville, Edison's Home. (502) 585-5247. Celebrate Thomas Edison's birthday with a visit to his Butchertown home full of artifacts and tales of little known facts. (first weekend in February).

BUFFALO DINNER AND NATIVE AMERICAN HERITAGE DAY

W - Gilbertsville, Kentucky Dam Village SRP. (270) 362-4271. Native American cultural demos, food and dance. (third Saturday in February).

MARCH

KENTUCKY HILLS WEEKEND

SE - Corbin, Cumberland Falls SRP. (800) 325-0063. Expressions of Appalachian culture through crafts, storytelling and music. (first weekend in March).

For updates visit our website: www.kidslovepublications.com

APRIL

EASTER CELEBRATIONS

Easter egg hunts, the Easter Bunny, Brunch Buffet and Sunrise Service. Also Most State Resort Parks. (Easter weekend)

❑   **NC** – Louisville. HAPPY EASTER BRUNCH CRUISE. Star of Louisville. (502) 589-7827 or **www.staroflouisville.com**.

❑   **NC** – New Haven. EASTER BUNNY EXPRESS. Kentucky RR Museum. (502) 549-5470. (weekend before Easter & Easter Saturday)

❑   **NE** – Ashland. EASTER EGG HUNT. Central Park. (606) 327-2046.

❑   **SE** – Richmond. EASTER EGG-STRAVAGANZA. Irvine McDowell Park. (800) 866-3705.

SOUTHERN KENTUCKY FESTIVAL OF BOOKS

SC – Bowling Green. (270) 745-5263 or **www.bookfest.org**. Tens of authors covering all subjects attend to autograph and discuss their books. Admission. (mid-April weekend)

HILLBILLY DAYS FESTIVAL

SE - Pikeville, downtown. (800) 844-7453. More than 60,000 people will show up for a fun look at the Hillbilly stereotype with food, a carnival, a parade and music that puts everyone in a "laid back" kind of mood. (mid-April for three days)

TATER DAY

W – Benton. (800) 467-7145. Thousands come to the annual celebration of the sweet potato featuring a carnival and baking competitions. (first Monday in April)

APRIL / MAY

KENTUCKY DERBY FESTIVAL

NC - Louisville. (800) 928-FEST. **www.kdf.org**. (mid-April thru first Saturday in May)

❑   **THUNDER OVER LOUISVILLE**, riverfront. The nation's largest fireworks and pyrotechnics display on earth (1 million people)! Also a great military air show. (mid-April Saturday)

❑   **GREAT BALLOON RACE**, Kentucky Fair and Exposition Center. Over 35 hot air balloons in the chase of the "hare" balloon. (last Saturday in April)

❑   **BEDLAM IN THE STREETS BED RACES**, Louisville Motor Speedway. Evening bed races. Corporate teams race in themed beds. Parade of beds at 6pm. (first Monday in May)

❑   **GREAT STEAMBOAT RACE**, riverfront. The race between the Belle of Louisville against a rival boat like the Delta Queen.

❑   **PEGASUS PARADE**, downtown. Spectacle of colorful floats, marching bands, giant inflatables, equestrians and celebrities starting west on Broadway. (first Thursday in May)

❑   **GOVERNOR'S DERBY BREAKFAST**, Capitol grounds, Frankfort. (800) 960-7200. Everyone is invited to the Capitol building for a free breakfast along with entertainment and crafts to enjoy afterwards. (morning of the 1st Saturday in May - Derby Day)

MAY

KENTUCKY SCOTTISH WEEKEND

NC - Carrollton, General Butler SRP. (502) 732-4384 or **www.kyscottishweekend.org**. The state celebrates many with Scottish heritage with athletic competitions, games, contests (how about the boniest knees contest?). Highland dancing and food. Saturday night Ceilidl and Sunday Kirkin' of the Tartan. Admission. (Mothers Day weekend in May)

For updates visit our website: www.kidslovepublications.com

MOTHER'S DAY EXPRESS

❑ **NC - New Haven,** Kentucky RR Museum. (800) 272-0152. Scenic train trip. Discounts for Moms with children. (Mother's Day)

❑ **NE – Versailles.** Bluegrass Scenic RR. (800) 755-2476 or **www.bgrm.org.**

THUNDERING EARTH POW-WOW

W – Hartford. (270) 274-9662. A traditional inter-tribal pow-wow with teepees set up and drummers. (second weekend in May)

INTERNATIONAL BAR-B-Q FESTIVAL

W - Owensboro, downtown. **www.bbqfest.com** or (800) 489-1131. Cooking teams compete to make the finest barbecued mutton, chicken and thousands of gallons of burgoo as judged and consumed by the public. Also games, contests and country dancing. (second weekend in May)

BATTLE OF SACRAMENTO

W - Sacramento. (270) 736-5114 or **www.baqttleofsac.com** This large re-enactment takes place on the original battlefield where Confederate Gen. Nathan Forrest and his bunch of 300 men won the day (Dec. 1861). (third weekend in May)

MEMORIAL DAY CELEBRATIONS

ALL AREAS - (800) 225-PARK. Most State Resort Parks provide entertainment and activities all weekend.

JUNE

CAPITAL EXPO FESTIVAL

NC - **Frankfort**, downtown. (502) 875-3524. Live entertainment, hot air balloon rides, fireworks and children's activities. (first full weekend in June)

OLD FORT HARROD HERITAGE FESTIVAL

NC - **Harrodsburg**, Old Fort Harrod State Park. (859) 734-3314. A celebration of state history and pioneer heritage with wagon rides, music, living history re-enactments of the fort's attack, craft demos and hands-on activities. (first full weekend in June)

SHAKERTOWN CIVIL WAR ENCAMPMENT

NC - **Harrodsburg**, Shaker Village of Pleasant Hill. (800) 734-5611. The Civil War as seen from the eyes of a strong, ritualistic religious community during this tumultuous period. (first weekend in June)

FATHER'S DAY EXCURSION

❑   NC - **New Haven**, Kentucky Railway Museum. (800) 272-0152. Fathers get 20% discount today.

❑   **NE – Versailles**. Bluegrass Scenic RR. (800) 755-2476 or **www.bgrm.org**.

MORGAN'S RAID ON GEORGETOWN

NE - **Georgetown**, Cardome Center. (502) 868-0975 or **www.morgansraid.com**. 500 re-enactors converge to take us all back to the days of the Civil War. Artillery night firings, military maneuvers and pioneer food. (second weekend in June)

FESTIVAL OF THE BLUEGRASS

NE - **Lexington**, Kentucky Horse Park. (800) 678-8813. The oldest bluegrass festival around with national bands (traditional, contemporary, ole tyme string style), workshops and kids activities. (second weekend in June-Thursday-Sunday)

For updates visit our website: www.kidslovepublications.com

DUNCAN HINES FESTIVAL

SC - Bowling Green. **www.duncanhinesfestival.com**. (270) 782-0800 or The native son of the famous baking products is honored with activities, food (especially desserts) and music. (second or third weekend in June)

GREAT AMERICAN BRASS BAND FESTIVAL

SC - Danville, Centre College Lawn. (800) 755-0076 or **www.gabbf.com**. "The most prominent and unusual musical festival in the country" is a FREE presentation of world-class bands. (second weekend in June)

CATCH A RAINBOW KIDS FISHING DERBY

SC - Jamestown, Wolf Creek Fish Hatchery. (270) 343-3797. Fishing derby for kids ages 0-15 with prizes and trophies awarded. (first Saturday in June)

GLASGOW HIGHLAND GAMES

SC - Lucas, Barren River Lake SRP. (800) 264-3161 or **www.glasgowhighlandgames.com**. A Scottish Heritage and Family Celebration with dancing , bagpipe and harp competition and children's games. (weekend after Memorial Day - Thursday-Sunday)

HATFIELD & MCCOY FESTIVAL

SE - Pikeville, downtown. (606) 432-5063. Light-hearted joking and fun surrounding the most famous feud in history. McCoys from all over the world and their invited guests (The Hatfields) will celebrate together. (second Saturday in June)

JEFFERSON DAVIS BIRTHDAY CELEBRATION

W - Fairview, Jefferson Davis State Historic Site. (270) 886-1765. A living history celebration honors the Confederate President on his birthday at his birthplace. The 351 foot obelisk is the 4th tallest in the world with an elevator to the top for viewing. (first weekend in June)

June *(cont.)*

W.C. HANDY BLUES AND BARBEQUE FESTIVAL

W - Henderson. (800) 648-3128 or **www.handyblues.org**. The legendary blues musician and composer is honored by his hometown community with jazz music and mouthwatering barbecue. (Entire second full week in June)

JULY

4TH OF JULY FESTIVALS

Fireworks, entertainment, parade and food!

- ❑ **ALL** – Most State Resort Parks. (800) 225-Park.
- ❑ **NC** – **Frankfort**. Riverfest. (800) 960-7200 or **www.visitfrankfort.com**.
- ❑ **NC** - **New Haven**, Kentucky Railway Museum. (800) 272-0152. (three days)
- ❑ **NE** – **Georgetown**. Downtown/Scott Cty. Park. (502) 863-2721.
- ❑ **NE** - **Lexington**, downtown. (859) 258-3100. Patriotic music concert, race, parade, fireworks and entertainment.
- ❑ **NE** – **Morehead**. Twin Knobs Beach/Cave Run Lake. (606) 784-6221.
- ❑ **NE** - **Versailles**, Woodford County Park. (859) 873-5122.
- ❑ **SC** - **Campbellsville**. (270) 465-8601. Battlefield ceremony of markers.
- ❑ **SE** - **Berea**. (859) 986-7710. Fireworks, kids activities, famous art demos of work in progress (years past it was sand art!).
- ❑ **SE** – **Clay City**. (606) 663-2224.
- ❑ **SE** - **Richmond**, Lake Reba Recreational Complex. (800) 866-3705.
- ❑ **W** – **Golden Pond**. Land Between the Lakes, The Homeplace. (800) 525-7077.
- ❑ **W** – **Hawesville**. Vastwood Park. (270) 927-8137. Fireworks on the lake with gospel singing , children's games, swimming and fishing.

For updates visit our website: www.kidslovepublications.com

4th of July Festivals *(cont.)*

- ❏ **W - Murray**. (800) 651-1603. Independence day with a community festival full of parades, concerts, fireworks and a street fair.
- ❏ **W - Owensboro**, English Park. (800) 489-1131. The conclusion of this festival is the fireworks display with accompaniment by the Symphony.
- ❏ **W – Paducah**. (270) 444-8508.

STEPHEN FOSTER-THE MUSICAL FOURTH OF JULY CELEBRATION

NC - **Bardstown**, My Old Kentucky Home SP. (800) 626-1563 or www.stephenfoster.com/july4.htm. Celebrate the birth of Foster, his music and our nation all in one night. Performance at 8:30pm with food, games and fireworks. (4th of July)

"SALUTE TO THE NATION" WORLD WAR II BATTLE REENACTMENT

NC - **Fort Knox**, Patton Museum. (270) 352-1204. Authentic American and German Vehicles and Uniforms with an Army Band concert. (4th of July)

A SHAKER FOURTH

NC - **Harrodsburg**, Shaker Village of Pleasant Hill. (800) 734-5611. Celebrate the fourth in the old-time Shaker Way. (4th of July)

WATERFRONT INDEPENDENCE FESTIVAL

NC - **Louisville**, Waterfront Park/Slugger Field. (502) 574-3768 or www.louisvillewaterfront.com. Live music, a RiverBats baseball game, children's activities, festival food and fireworks extravaganza. Star of Louisville Fireworks Cruises. (around July 4th)

SUMMER MOTION

NE - **Ashland**, Central Park and Riverfront. (800) 377-6249. 4th of July five day celebration is a huge party with fireworks, concerts, food, etc. (first five days of July)

July *(cont.)*

BLUEGRASS STATE GAMES

NE - Lexington. (859) 255-0336 or **www.wgsg.org**. Kentucky's premier amateur   athletic competition for participants and spectators. (last two weekends in July)

BALLOON CLASSIC

SC - Bowling Green. (270) 745-7509. Over 60 hot air balloons will fill the sky over town. Run by a Missionary group, many of the balloons are images of Jesus or Noah's Ark. Very fun and different, endearing sights towards the heavens. (third or fourth weekend in July)

LAKEFEST

SC - Jamestown, Lake Cumberland. (270) 343-4594. Fun family festival. (first weekend in July)

BEREA CRAFT AND INTERNATIONAL FOLK FESTIVALS

SE - Berea, throughout downtown and Indian Fort Theatre. (800) 598-5263. Voted the top 20 events in the southeast, there are usually over 125 artists from around the country demonstrating and selling their workmanship. International music, dance and theater are a wonderful compliment. (mid-July weekend)

AUGUST

LIVING HISTORY AND CIVIL WAR SHOW

NC - Bardstown, Civil War Museum. (502) 349-0291. Drills portraying the Battle of Bardstown in the Civil War. Soldiers in uniform and ladies in period costume. (first full weekend in August)

PIONEER DAYS

NC - Harrodsburg. (800) 355-9192 or www.pioneerdays.org. Kentucky's first settlement celebrates its history and heritage with food, square dancing, clogging, flint rock rifle shot contest and demonstrations. (third weekend in August)

KENTUCKY STATE FAIR

NC - Louisville, Kentucky Fair and Exposition Center. (502) 367-5000 or www.kyfairexpo.org. "Everybody's State Fair" offers over a dozen stages featuring many big name concerts, 10,000 animals, "thrillway" rides, World Championship Horse Show, senior and children's entertainment. (mid-August to late-August for 11 days)

KIDS WEEKEND

NE - Lexington, Kentucky Horse Park. (859) 233-4303. Beginners luck - hands-on with horses, treasure hunts, stick horse riding, horseshoe painting, children's horse shows, and storytelling. Admission. (first full weekend in August)

BATTLE OF BLUE LICKS RE-ENACTMENT

NE - Mt. Olivet, Blue Licks Battlefield SRP. (859) 289-5507. The very last battle of the Revolutionary War is acted out with some light-hearted fun plus realistic living history. Period music and food served up, too. (3rd weekend in August)

STANTON CORN FESTIVAL

NE - Stanton, Stanton City Park. (606) 663-2271. Quaint corn festival with corn foods and music in the heart of the Red River Gorge. (early August)

BATTLE OF MIDDLE CREEK

SE - Prestonsburg. (606) 886-1341. Future President James A. Garfield commanded the Union troops at this battle on January 10, 1862. It ended up being the largest battle in Eastern Kentucky. Technically a draw, but the Confederate troops retreated. See a re-enactment. (August)

August *(cont.)*

WESTERN KENTUCKY STATE FAIR

W - Hopkinsville. Fairgrounds Park. (800) 842-9959. Live entertainment, truck & tractor pulls, demo derby, livestock and a midway of rides. (first long weekend in August)

FANCY FARM PICNIC

W – Mayfield. www.kentuckylakebarkley.org. Guinness Book of World Records – World's Largest Picnic. (first Saturday in August)

AUGUST 8TH EMANCIPATION CELEBRATION

W - Paducah. (800) PADUCAH. The town's African-American community celebrates with a memorial service, food, parade and lots of activity centers. (first full week in August)

SEPTEMBER

KENTUCKY FOLKLIFE FESTIVAL

NC - Frankfort, downtown. (877) 444-7867 or **www.folklife.ky.gov**. Celebrate Kentucky folklife with updated demonstrations and exhibits designed to educate and entertain visitors to Kentucky culture, food and musical heritage. Family Folklore tent on the river has many hands-on activities. "A Chance to Dance" teaches visitors new ethnic moves. (last weekend in September)

19TH CENTURY COUNTRY FAIR

NC - Harrodsburg, Shaker Village of Pleasant Hill. (800) 734-5611. Fall harvest event is reminiscent of an old time country fair. (fourth weekend in September)

BURGOO FESTIVAL

NC - Lawrenceburg. (502) 839-6959. A competition and tasting of the stew made with unusual and flavorful ingredients. "Everything but the kitchen sink" is the centerpiece of this tasty festival. (last long weekend in September)

OKTOBERFEST

NE - Covington, MainStrasse Village. (859) 491-0458. Fall celebration with traditional German accent on food and games. (weekend after Labor Day)

HARVEST FESTIVAL

NE - Georgetown, Quest Farm. (502) 535-6064 or **www.questfarm.org.** Music, horseback riding, hayrides and good fall food. (2nd Sunday in September)

HARVEST FESTIVAL

NE - Morehead. (800) 654-1944. Celebrate the bountiful Kentucky harvest with bluegrass music, food, hayrides and train rides. (third weekend in September)

CAVE RUN STORYTELLING FESTIVAL

NE - Morehead. (800) 654-1944. Nationally known storytellers tell their tales in a scenic setting. (fourth weekend in September)

SORGHUM FESTIVAL

NE – Morgan County Fairgrounds. (606) 743-3330. Mule-drawn cane mill, traditional food, craft demos, parade and live music. (fourth weekend in September)

DANIEL BOONE PIONEER FESTIVAL

NE - Winchester, College Park. (800) 298-9105. Visit the Old Stone Church where the Boone's attended along with celebrating the Boone heritage with national entertainment, fireworks and a dance. (Labor Day weekend - Friday-Monday)

September *(cont.)*

APPLE CIDER SIPPIN' CELEBRATION

SC - Bowling Green, 101 Claypool-Alvaton Road (corner KY 234 & 961). **http://members.aol.com/bappfarm/bromer.htm**. (270) 782-9243. Drive out to the country to purchase freshly picked apples or warm fried apple pie or fresh squeezed apple cider. Pick-u-own and special weekends with apple themes. (entire month of September)

APPLE FESTIVAL

SC - Casey County Fairgrounds. **www.theapplefestival.com**. (606) 787-8177. The world's largest apple pie is complemented by a parade, apple foods, music, contests and fireworks. (very last weekend in September)

CONSTITUTION SQUARE FESTIVAL

SC - Danville, Constitution Square State Historical Site, downtown. (859) 239-7089. Celebrate where Kentucky's Statehood began with a visit to the first Post Office west of the Alleghenies, a jail, the courthouse and the meeting house. The site is set up as life was 200 years ago with arts and crafts demos, living history actors and entertainment. (third weekend in September)

COUNTRY HAM DAYS

SC - Lebanon. (270) 692-9594 or **www.hamdays.com**. Over 600 hams are prepared to serve with Southern style side dishes. Cloggers, line dances, steam engine show, Pokey Pig Run and entertainment. (fourth weekend in September)

WATERMELON FESTIVAL

SC - Monroe County Fairgrounds. (270) 487-5504. Rolley-hole Marble (hand-made flint) tournaments, watermelon-related competitions (greased watermelon carry or seed spitting contests), live music and a street dance. (Labor Day Saturday)

SPOONBREAD FESTIVAL

SE - Berea. (859) 986-9760. This festival honors the famous bread served at Boone Tavern. Check out the spoonbread eating contest, live music, children's activities, food and hot air balloons. (second weekend in September)

BLACK GOLD FESTIVAL

SE - Hazard. (606) 436-0161. Coal is honored with amusements, great mountain food, a parade and a coal truck competition. (mid-September)

WORLD CHICKEN FESTIVAL

SE - London, downtown. www.chickenfestival.com. (800) 348-0095. You are egg-spected for this good time complete with a gander at the World's Largest Skillet, entertainment and rides. It celebrates the county where the first Kentucky Fried Chicken was established. Come with an appetite! (last full weekend in September - Thursday-Sunday)

EVERLY BROTHERS HOMECOMING

W - Central City. (270) 754-9603. Don and Phil Everly host a grand concert. Bring lawn chairs and blankets. (Labor Day weekend)

TRAIL OF TEARS INDIAN POW-WOW

W - Hopkinsville, Trail of Tears Park (US 41/9th St. & Skyline Drive). (800) 842-9959. A sad period in our country's history is remembered with tribal dancing, Native American storytelling and food. Meet Chiefs Whitepath and Fly Smith and stop in the Heritage Museum (open Tuesday-Saturday 10:00am-2:00pm year round) to view cultural displays. (weekend after Labor Day)

ANTIQUE GAS AND STEAM ENGINE SHOW

W – Paducah, Carson Park. (270) 554-3246. Antique cars, tractors and engines, tractor pulls, wheat threshing, pulling teams, parades, arts & crafts, barbecue and music. (third weekend in September)

September *(cont.)*

CIVIL WAR HISTORY WEEKEND

W - Paducah, Schultz Park and Tilghman Civil War Museum. (800) PADUCAH. Living history commemorating the 1864 Battle of Paducah. Commemorative talk and interpretive walking tour, firing demonstrations, living history demonstrations of Civil War soldiers. (second weekend in September)

FESTIVAL OF MURALS AND ARTS IN ACTION

W - Paducah. (800) PADUCAH. Paducah celebrates its history as the floodwall murals are "brought to life" in living history performances. Demonstrating artists, arts and crafts sales, live music and dance performances, games, hay rides, Taste of Paducah, free Quilt Museum and gallery admission. (last weekend in September)

OFFICIAL KENTUCKY LABOR DAY PARADE

W - Paducah. (800) PADUCAH. Celebration includes live entertainment, a barbeque and the parade. (Labor Day weekend)

WESTERN KENTUCKY HIGHLAND FESTIVAL

W – Paducah, Carson Park Fairgrounds. (270) 443-2064. Celebrate the Celtic heritage with pipe and drum bands, dancers, athletes, and children's activities. (second Saturday in September)

SEPTEMBER / OCTOBER

MAZE CRAZE

NC – Leitchfield. Hopewell Heritage Farm. (270) 879-4023. Hay maze, hayrides to field. Admission. (September/October)

AUTUMNFEST

NE - Georgetown, Bi-Water Farm (US 25N). (502) 863-3676. Farm festival full of color and fall food and hayrides. (fourth weekend in September thru October)

For updates visit our website: www.kidslovepublications.com

FESTIVAL OF THE HORSE

NE - Georgetown. (502) 863-2547. Central Kentucky's premiere horse festival with a family orientation featuring entertainment, food, a children's parade and of course, a horse show. (end of September beginning of October weekend)

PUMPKIN FEST

NE - Georgetown, Double Stink Hog Farm (I-75exit 126, US 460E & KY 922). (502) 868-9703. A festival famous for their down-home country festivals with u-pick pumpkins, food, a petting zoo and hayrides. (last weekend in September and first weekend in October)

SORGHUM FESTIVAL

NE – Gladie Creek, Historic Site, Red River Gorge. (606) 663-2852. A harvest farm festival where the old cane mill is running, turning raw plant into sticky sweet sorghum. Music and food add to the farm setting charm. (late September, early October weekend)

PUMPKIN FESTIVAL

NE - Maysville, "R" Farm, 7172 Strodes Run Rd. (606) 742-2429. (last weekend in September, first weekend in October)

SIEGE OF BOONESBOROUGH 1778 REENACTMENT

SE – Richmond. Fort Boonesborough. (859) 527-3131. A living history presentation and reenactment of the "Great Siege" of September 1778. (last weekend in September)

OCTOBER

WATSON'S PUMPKIN PATCH FESTIVAL

NC - Bardstown, Watson's Farm. (502) 252-7212. Fall favorites like hayrides, a hay maze, carnival rides, sorghum making, homemade food and pony rides. (first and second weekend in October)

October *(cont.)*

TWO RIVERS FESTIVAL

NC - Carrollton, confluence of the Kentucky and Ohio Rivers. (502) 732-5713 or **www.tworiversfest.com**. Fall festival with all of a rivertown flare. (first weekend in October)

GREAT PUMPKIN FESTIVAL

NC - Frankfort. (502) 223-2261. Harvest season with hayrides, children's activities, costume parade down Main Street, pumpkin decorating and live entertainment. (third weekend in October)

LINCOLN DAYS CELEBRATION

NC - Hodgenville. (270) 358-3411. Honoring native son Abraham Lincoln with a Lincoln Look Alike and Mary Todd Lincoln contests, antique costume contests, pioneer games and railsplitting tournaments. (second weekend in October)

COLORFEST

NC - Louisville, Bernheim Forest. (502) 955-8512 or **www.bernheim.org/colorfest.htm**. Fall festival featuring craft and nature exhibits for children, food, storytelling, music and activities. Hay Maze, paint pumpkins, puppet shows and hayrides. Admission per vehicle. (third weekend in October)

SORGHUM FESTIVAL

NC - Springfield. (859) 336-3810. A fall harvest festival with agricultural products and farmers featured in areas of craft, food, and contests. (early October weekend)

KENTUCKY WOOL FESTIVAL

NE - Falmouth. (859) 654-3378. Once a strong area sheep industry town, now the area maintains its heritage with demos on sheep shearing and sheep dog herding, wool spinning, sorghum and corn products, ethnic foods and a petting zoo. (second weekend in October)

BIG BONE LICK SALT FESTIVAL

NE - Union, Big Bone Lick SP. (859) 384-3522. A festival devoted to exploring the significance of area salt licks to early pioneers with demos and crafts. (first long weekend in October)

FALL FESTIVAL

NE – Williamstown. Farmer Bills and MamMaws Kitchen. 1790 Baton Rouge Road (I-75 exit 154). (800) 382-7117. Pumpkin patch, corn maze, petting zoo and harvest foods. (October)

PUMPKIN FESTIVAL

SC - Edmonton. (270) 432-3561. Area grown prize pumpkins are weighed, carved and cooked to make fall crafts and food. (first Saturday in October)

GREAT OUTHOUSE BLOWOUT

SC – Gravel Switch, Penn's Store. (859) 332-7715. The annual memorial tribute to the 1992 Penn's Privy Dedication (gained national attention the year they first installed an outhouse). Featuring the "Outhouse 300" where teams race the 300 foot course, pushing and pulling their "designer outhouses" on wheels for the "gold" in outhouse racing. Also see the Parade of Privies, music, outhouse memorabilia and great food. Fee for parking. (first Saturday in October)

COLORFALL

SC - Mammoth Cave National Park. (270) 758-2254. A wonderful addition to your family "cave" experience celebrating the cultural heritage of this region with storytelling and archeological demos. (second week in October)

PERRYVILLE BATTLEFIELD COMMEMORATION

SC - Perryville Battlefield SHS. (859) 332-8631. Living history exhibits and battle re-enactments honor the worst of Kentucky's Civil War battles with encampments, sutters and music. Parking fee. (first full weekend in October)

October *(cont.)*

HARVEST FESTIVAL

SC - Russell Springs. Veterans Fairgrounds. (270) 343-3191. Fall harvest-time is here and the area's fresh produce is displayed and sold here along with fall crafts, food and entertainment. (first Saturday in October)

WOOLY WORM FESTIVAL

SE - Beattyville. (606) 464-2888. A unique annual celebration of the predictor of coming winter weather with announcement of results of a survey sent to the National Weather Service along with crafts, entertainment and a wooly worm race (as the fans cheer them on!). (third weekend in October)

CAMP WILDCAT RE-ENACTMENT

SE - London, Wildcat Mountain. (606) 528-1817. The Civil War battle of Wildcat is re-enacted as the first Union victory of the War (along Wilderness Road) with living history exhibits. (third weekend in October)

CUMBERLAND MOUNTAIN FALL FESTIVAL

SE - Middlesboro and Cumberland Gap NHP. (800) 988-1075 or **www.thefallfestival.com**. Old English pioneer heritage through the gap is celebrated with live pioneer demos, crafts, food and entertainment. (first weekend in October)

KENTUCKY APPLE FESTIVAL

SE - Paintsville. (800) 542-5790. The orchards are harvested and the products honored with apple foods and crafts, amusement rides, a parade, square dancing and clogging and live entertainment. (first week in October)

APPALACHIAN HARVEST FESTIVAL

SE - Renfro Valley. (800) 765-7464. Fall harvest-time with an old fashioned flare including molasses made from a mule-drawn press, antique farm machinery, music and a covered-wagon train. (first weekend in October)

For updates visit our website: www.kidslovepublications.com

FIDDLERS FESTIVAL

SE - Renfro Valley. (800) 765-7464. Toe-tapping fun as fiddlers from around the country get together to perform and just jam. (last weekend in October)

KIDSDAYS

SE - Richmond, Lake Reba Recreation Complex. (800) 866-3705. A carnival and activities totally devoted to kids having fun. (second long weekend in October, Wednesday-Sunday)

HAM FESTIVAL

W – Cadiz. (888) 446-6402. Highlight is cooking of the world's largest ham and biscuit sandwich (Guinness Record). Top name performers and food. (second weekend in October)

CIVIL WAR DAYS

W - Columbus, Columbus-Belmont SP. (270) 677-2327. The living history presentations portray Grant's first assignment at a strategic location for control of the Mississippi River. They formed a Confederate "chain of men" and this is re-enacted. Authentic sutlers, music, food. Night firing of the cannons and Sunday church services. (second weekend in October)

SORGHUM FESTIVAL

W – Hawesville. Fairgrounds. (270) 314-5688 or (270) 927-8137. Sorghum making and sampling. Food, arts/crafts, rug and basket weavers. (second weekend in October)

APPLE FESTIVAL

W - Owensboro, Reid's Orchard (KY 144). (270) 685-2444 or **www.visitowensboro.com**. An abundance of apples are featured in a carnival, crafts, petting zoo, hayrides, pick-u-own and apple food and cider. (third weekend in October)

NOVEMBER

FT. HARROD HOLIDAY GALA

NC - Harrodsburg, Old Ft. Harrod SP. (859) 734-3314. A Victorian open house celebration with a Christmas tree festival and Mr. & Mrs. Claus. Small admission. (weekend before Thanksgiving in November)

KENTUCKY BOOK FAIR

NC – Frankfort. Kentucky State University Exum Center. www.kybookfair.com. Books about Kentucky or authors from Kentucky. Workshops and autographings make for good Christmas gifts. (first Saturday in November)

NOVEMBER / DECEMBER

SANTA EXPRESS

Train rides with Santa and treats.

- ❏ **NC - New Haven**, Kentucky Railway Museum. (800) 272-0152 (first weekend in December and every weekend until Christmas)
- ❏ **NE - Versailles**, Bluegrass Scenic RR. (800) 755-2476 or www.bgrm.org. (Thanksgiving-December)
- ❏ **W – Hardin**, Hardin Southern Railroad. (270) 437-4555 or www.hsrr.com. Cars not heated, dress for weather.

CHRISTMAS OPEN HOUSES

A great family time to visit many elaborate homes that may be too stuffy or boring to tour (for kids) any other time of year. Open houses generally have extensive holiday decorations, music and refreshments served. Admission is charged.

- ❏ **NC - Bardstown**, My Old Kentucky Home. (800) 323-7803. Candlelight tours with elaborate period costumes and horse-drawn carriages. (Thanksgiving weekend thru second Saturday in December)

For updates visit our website: www.kidslovepublications.com

Christmas Open Houses *(cont.)*

❑ **NC – Carrollton,** General Butler State Park. **www.kystateparks.com/genbutlr.htm**. Butler-Turpin Historic House - A Patriotic Christmas. Festival of Trees, Santa and horse-drawn carriages. Admission. (Thanksgiving weekend to mid-December)

❑ **NC - Louisville,** Edison's House. (502) 585-5247. (first Saturday in December)

❑ **NE – Burlington,** Dinsmore Farm. Christmas in the Country. (859)586-6117 or **www.dinsmorefarm.org**. (first long full weekend in December)

❑ **NE - Lexington,** Ashland, Henry Clay Estate. (859) 266-8581. Civil War Christmas. (second weekend in December)

❑ **NE - Lexington,** Waveland SHS. (859) 272-3611. Candlelight tours. (second weekend in December)

❑ **SC - Bowling Green,** Riverview at Hobson Grove. (270) 843-5565. Southern Kentucky Victorian style tours. (last week of Nov - just before Christmas)

❑ **SC - Danville,** McDowell House. (800) 755-0076. (first full weekend in December)

❑ **SC – Stanford,** W. Whitley House State Historic Site. Pioneer Christmas Candlelight. (606) 355-2885.

❑ **W – Golden Pond,** Land Between the Lakes & The Homeplace. (270) 924-2000 or (800) LBL-7077. (Thanksgiving time)

FESTIVAL OF LIGHTS

❑ **NC – Elizabethtown,** Christmas in Freeman Lake Park. (800) 437-0092.

❑ **NC – Louisville.** Jefferson Square. (502) 568-7000. The switch is thrown at dusk (~7:40pm) to illuminate downtown with over 40 buildings covered in holiday lights. There's also Santa's arrival, fireworks, a global village, entertainment throughout the day, and a children's holiday parade in the daytime. Brunch with Santa & Animals at the Zoo runs weekends in December. (begins the day after Thanksgiving thru December)

Festival of Lights *(cont.)*

- ❑ **NE - Ashland**, Winter Wonderland of Lights. (800) 377-6249 or **www.winterwonderland.org**. 700,000 plus lights of 35 displays seen by carriage ride through community with centerpiece at Central Park. Also activity at Highland Museum & Festival of Trees. (mid-November thru New Years Eve)

- ❑ **NE - Lexington**, Southern Lights, Kentucky Horse Park. (800) 678-8813. With the Horse Park setting, drive thru 2.5 miles of animated displays of lighted holiday cartoon characters, many equine-themed action scenes, Cinderella's carriage and dinosaurs. Santa, mini-trains, performers, snacks and hot beverages are available too. Nightly 5:30-10:00pm. Admission per carload approx. $12.00. (Saturday before Thanksgiving - December)

- ❑ **NE - Mt. Sterling**, Christmas in the Park, Easy Walker Park. (859) 498-8732. A walking tour of a park aglow with over 60 decorated trees and 10,000 lights. (week of Thanksgiving - New Year's Day)

- ❑ **SC - Bowling Green**, Winter Lights, Basil Griffin Park. (270) 782-3660. Car drive thru huge light displays. (late November - New Year's Eve)

- ❑ **SC - Burnside**, Christmas Island, General Burnside Island SP. (800) 642-6287. One million lights on this 3.5 mile tour through a wonderland of 200 lighted displays. Horse-drawn carriage rides. (weekend before Thanksgiving - day before New Year's Eve)

- ❑ **SE – Breaks**, Interstate Park. Mountain Top Christmas Lights. (800) 982-5122 or **www.tourpikecounty.com**.

- ❑ **SE – Harlan,** Holiday Lights and Christmas Village. (606) 573-4156. (Thanksgiving thru New Years weekend)

- ❑ **SE - Hazard**, Christmas in Perry County Park. (606) 439-2659. Drive-through of wonderful lights that make the town look like the North Pole. (Thanksgiving-time - Christmas Day)

- ❑ **SE - Renfro Valley**, Christmas in the Valley. (800) 765-7464. One of Kentucky's largest light displays, performances and special holiday shopping. (weekend before Thanksgiving - mid December)

Festival of Lights *(cont.)*

- ❑ **SE - Richmond**, Hummel Planetarium, Story of A Star. (859) 622-1547. (Thanksgiving weekend - December)
- ❑ **W – Henderson**, Central Park. Christmas in the Park. (800) 648-3128. Life-size toys, Santa and evening Fantasy of Lights. (December)
- ❑ **W – Owensboro**, Holiday in the Park. Legion Park. (270) 687-8700. (December)

CHRISTMAS PARADES

- ❑ **NC – Harrodsburg**. (859) 734-4394. (first Saturday in December)
- ❑ **NE – Ashland**. (606) 324-5111. (Tuesday before Thanksgiving)
- ❑ **NE – Georgetown**. (502) 863-5424. (weekend after Thanksgiving)
- ❑ **NE – Lexington**. (859) 231-7335. (first Saturday in December)
- ❑ **NE – Maysville**. (606) 564-9419. (first Friday evening in December)
- ❑ **NE – Mt. Sterling**. (859) 498-8732. (first Saturday in December)
- ❑ **NE - Versailles**. (859) 873-5122. (first Saturday in December)
- ❑ **SC - Edmonton**. (270) 432-3222. (second Saturday in December)
- ❑ **SC - Somerset**. (606) 679-7323. (first Saturday in December)
- ❑ **SE - London**, downtown. (606) 878-6900. (first Saturday in December)
- ❑ **SE - Richmond**. (800) 866-3705. (first weekend in December)
- ❑ **SE - Harlan**. (606) 573-4717. (first Saturday in December)
- ❑ **W – Central City**. Kentucky's Largest Small Town Christmas Parade. (270) 754-2360. (Thanksgiving Day)
- ❑ **W – Hopkinsville**. (800) 909-9016. (Saturday in December)
- ❑ **W - Marion**. (270) 965-5015. (second Saturday in December)
- ❑ **W – Owensboro**. (270) 683-2060. (mid-November)
- ❑ **W - Paducah**. (800) PADUCAH. (first Saturday in December)

DECEMBER

BETHLEHEM LIVING NATIVITY

NC - Bethlehem. (502) 845-5046. A still scene depicting the Christmas story with live characters and animals. (four days before and including Christmas)

SHAKER ORDER OF CHRISTMAS

NC - Harrodsburg, Shaker Village of Pleasant Hill. Partake in viewing Shaker traditions in music and decorations and community caroling. (first full week in December beginning Saturday)

CHRISTMAS ON THE FARM

NE - Corinth, Mullins Log Cabin. (859) 824-0565. An old-fashioned country gathering with craft demos and wagon rides and warm food. (first weekend in December)

NEW YEARS EVE CELEBRATIONS

No alcohol, "First Night" themed, family-friendly evening activities and party with live entertainment all the way past midnight!

- ❑ **State Resort Parks** (some, check for content on website). (800) 225-PARK. Reservations needed.
- ❑ **NE - Ashland**, Judd Plaza. (800) 377-6249.

Master
Index

For updates visit our website: www.kidslovepublications.com

Activity Index

PROUDLY

MADE IN THE USA

AMUSEMENTS

NC - Louisville, *Six Flags Kentucky Kingdom*, 35

SC - Bowling Green, *Beech Bend Park*, 73

SC - Bowling Green, *Russell Sims Aquatic Center*, 76

SC - Cave City, *Big Mike's Mystery House*, 80

SC - Cave City, *Dinosaur Wld*, 81

SC - Cave City, *Guntown Mountain*, 81

SC - Cave City, *Kentucky Action Park And Jesse James Riding Stables*, 82

SC - Cave City, *Mammoth Cave Jellystone Park Camp Resort*, 83

SC - Cave City, *Wigwam Village*, 84

SE - Williamsburg, *Kentucky Splash Water Park*, 122

W - Dunmor, *Dogwood Lakes Resort & Funpark*, 127

W - Eddyville, *Venture River Water Park*, 128

ANIMALS & FARMS

NC - Frankfort, *Buckley Wildlife Sanctuary*, 10

NC - Frankfort, *Salato Wildlife Education Center*, 16

NC - Louisville, *Louisville Zoo*, 33

NC - Prospect, *Henry's Ark*, 37

NC - Shelbyville, *Buffalo Crossing*, 38

NE - Lexington, *Kentucky Horse Park*, 55

NE - Lexington, *Raven Run Nature Sanctuary*, 57

NE - Morehead, *Minor Clark State Fish Hatchery*, 60

NE - Newport, *Newport Aquarium*, 62

SC - Horse Cave, *Kentucky Down Under / Kentucky Caverns*, 89

SE - Richmond, *Lou-Ron Horse Show Center*, 117

SE - Slade, *Kentucky Reptile Zoo*, 119

KENTUCKY HISTORY

NC - Bedford, *Trimble County Old Stone Jail & County Courthouse*, 6

NC - Elizabethtown, *Historic Downtown Elizabethtown Walking Tour*, 8

NC - Frankfort, *Executive Mansion*, 10

NC - Frankfort, *Kentucky History Center*, 11

NC - Frankfort, *Kentucky Military History Museum*, 12

NC - Frankfort, *Kentucky State Capitol Area*, 12

NC - Frankfort, *Kentucky Vietnam Veteran's Memorial*, 13

NC - Frankfort, *Leslie Morris Park On Fort Hill*, 14

NC - Frankfort, *Lt. Governor's Mansion*, 14

NC - Frankfort, *Old State Capitol*, 14

NC - Harrodsburg, *Old Fort Harrod State Park*, 19

NC - Hodgenville, *Abraham Lincoln Birthplace National Historic Site*, 20

NC - Hodgenville, *Lincoln's Boyhood Home*, 21

NC - La Grange, *Oldham County History Center*, 22

NC - Louisville, *Locust Grove Historic Home*, 30

MUSEUMS *(cont.)*

NE - Lexington, *Parkette Drive-In*, 50

NE - Lexington, *Lexington Children's Museum*, 53

NE - Lexington, *Hunt-Morgan House*, 54

NE - Lexington, *Waveland State Historic Site*, 56

NE - Lexington, *Aviation Museum Of Kentucky*, 57

NE - Lexington, *Keeneland Track Kitchen*, 58

NE - Maysville, *National Underground Railroad*, 59

NE - Nicholasville, *Harry Miller Lock Collection*, 63

NE - Paris, *Hopewell Museum*, 65

NE - Versailles, *Jouett House*, 66

NE - Versailles, *Nostalgia Station Toy & Train*, 67

NE - Washington, *Harriet Beecher Stowe Slavery To Freedom Museum*, 67

SC - Bowling Green, *BRIMS - Barren River Imaginative Museum Of Science*, 74

SC - Bowling Green, *National Corvette Museum*, 75

SC - Cave City, *Floyd Collins*, 81

SC - Cave City, *Mammoth Cave Wax Museum*, 83

SC - Cave City, *Mammoth Cave Wildlife Museum*, 84

SC - Danville, *McDowell House And Apothecary*, 85

SC - Gravel Switch, *Penn's Store*, 87

SE - Benham, *Kentucky Coal Mining Museum*, 101

SE - Corbin, *Harland Sanders Café & Museum*, 105

SE - Elkhorn City, *Elkhorn City Railroad Museum*, 106

SE - Harlan, *Pine Mountain Settlement*, 107

SE - Hindman, *Hindman Settlement School*, 108

SE - Hyden, *Frontier Nursing Service*, 108

SE - Middlesboro, *Bell County Historical Museum & Coal House*, 110

SE - Middlesboro, *Lost Squadron Museum*, 111

SE - Renfro Valley, *Kentucky Music Hall Of Fame*, 114

SE - Van Lear, *Van Lear Historical Society Coal Camp Museum*, 121

W - Fort Campbell, *Pratt Memorial, Don F.*, 129

W - Grand Rivers, *Patti's 1880's Settlement*, 132

W - Guthrie, *Robert Penn Warren Birthplace*, 133

W - Marion, *Clement Mineral*, 136

W - Owensboro, *Owensboro Museum Of Science And History*, 138

W - Owensboro, *Int'l Bluegrass Music Museum*, 138

W - Paducah, *Civil War Museum - Tilghman*, 139

W - Paducah, *National Quilt*, 139

W - Paducah, *River Heritage & Floodwall Murals*, 140

W - Paducah, *William Clark Market House Museum*, 141

W - Princeton, *Adsmore House*, 142

OUTDOORS

NC - Carrollton, *General Butler State Resort Park*, 6

NC - Clermont, *Bernheim Forest*, 7

NC - Fairdale, *Jefferson Memorial Forest*, 36

For updates visit our website: www.kidslovepublications.com

OUTDOORS (cont.)

W - Dunmor, *Lake Malone SP*, 128
W - Eddyville, *Mineral Mound State Park*, 128
W - Fairview, *Jefferson Davis Monument Historic Site*, 129
W - Gilbertsville, *Kentucky Dam Village*, 130
W - Gilbertsville, *Maggie's Jungle Golf*, 131
W - Golden Pond, *Land Between The Lakes Nat'l Recreation Area*, 131
W - Hardin, *Kenlake State Resort Park*, 134
W - Henderson, *John James Audubon State Park*, 135
W - Hopkinsville, *Trail Of Tears Commemorative Park*, 136
W - Owensboro, *Ben Hawes State Park*, 137
W - Wickliffe, *Wickliffe Mounds*, 143

SPORTS

NC - Louisville, *Louisville Motor Speedway*, 34
NC - Louisville, *Louisville River Bats*, 35
NC - Sparta, *Kentucky Speedway*, 39
NE - Georgetown, *Cincinnati Bengals Summer Training Camp*, 48
NE - Lexington, *Lexington Legends Baseball*, 53
SE - London, *Daniel Boone Motocross Park*, 108
SE - Richmond, *Richmond Raceway*, 118
W - Calvert City, *Kentucky Lake Motor Speedway*, 125
W - Paducah, *Paducah International Raceway*, 140

THE ARTS

NC - Bardstown, *Stephen Foster - The Musical*, 5
NC - Frankfort, *Country Place Jamboree*, 10
NC - Harrodsburg, *Daniel Boone, The Man & The Legend*, 18
NC - Hodgenville, *Lincoln Jamboree*, 20
NC - Louisville, *Louisville Ballet*, 24
NC - Louisville, *Stage One - Louisville Children's Theatre*, 26
NC - Louisville, *Speed Art Museum*, 32
NC - Louisville, *Music Theatre Louisville*, 34
NC - West Point, *Music Ranch USA*, 40
NE - Covington, *Carnegie Visual & Performing Arts Center*, 45
NE - Covington, *Mainstrasse Village*, 45
NE - Lexington, *Central Kentucky Youth Orchestra*, 52
NE - Lexington, *Lexington Children's Theatre*, 52
NE - Lexington, *Lexington Philharmonic*, 53
NE - Lexington, *Lexington Ballet*, 53
NE - Morehead, *Kentucky Folk Art Center*, 59
SC - Bowling Green, *Capitol Arts Center*, 77
SC - Brownsville, *Floyd Collins Story Outdoor Drama*, 78
SC - Danville, *Pioneer Playhouse*, 86
SC - Lebanon, *Hoofprints On The Stairs*, 90
SE - Clay City, *Meadowgreen Park Bluegrass Music Hall*, 104

For updates visit our website: www.kidslovepublications.com

Travel Journal & Notes:

Travel Journal & Notes:

Travel Journal & Notes:

Travel Journal & Notes:

Travel Journal & Notes:

Travel Journal & Notes:

GROUP DISCOUNTS &
FUNDRAISING OPPORTUNITIES!

We're excited to introduce our books to your group! These guides for parents, grandparents, teachers and visitors are great tools to help you discover hundreds of fun places to visit. Our titles are great resources for all the wonderful places to travel either locally or across the region.

We are two parents who have researched, written and published these books. We have spent thousands of hours collecting information and *personally traveled over 20,000 miles* visiting all of the most unique places listed in our guides. The books are kid-tested and the descriptions include great hints on what kids like best!

Please consider the following Group Purchase options: *For the latest information, visit our website:* **www.kidslovepublications.com**

❑ **Group Discount/Fundraising** – Purchase books at the discount price of $2.95 off the suggested retail price for members/friends. Minimum order is ten books. You may mix titles to reach the minimum order. Greater discounts (~35%) are available for fundraisers. Minimum order is thirty books. Call for details.

❑ **Available for Interview/Speaking** – The authors have a treasure bag full of souvenirs from favorite places. We'd love to share ideas on planning fun trips to take children while exploring your home state. The authors are available, by appointment, *(based on availability)* at (614) 792-6451 or **michele@kidslovepublications.com**. A modest honorarium or minimum group sale purchase will apply. Call or visit our website for details.

Call us soon at (614) 792-6451 to make arrangements!
Happy Exploring!

YOUR FAMILY MEMORIES!

Now that you've created memories with your family,

it's time to keepsake them by scrapbooking

in this unique, family-friendly way!

Check Out These Unique Features:

* **The Book That Shrinks As It Grows!** - Specially designed pages can be removed as you add pictures to your book. This keeps your unique travel journal from becoming too thick to use.

* **Write Your Own Book** - The travel journal is designed to get you started and help you remember those great family fun times!

* **Design Your Own Book** - Most illustrations and picture frames are designed to encourage kids to color them.

* **Unique Chapter Names** - help you <u>simply</u> categorize your family travel memories.

* **Acid Free Paper** - was used to print your book to keep your photos safe for a lifetime!

Writing Your Own Family Travel Book is This Easy...

**Step 1 - Select, Cut and Paste
Your Favorite Travel Photos**

**Step 2 - Color the Fun
Theme Picture Frames**

**Step 3 - Write about Your
Travel Stories in the Journal
(We get you started...)**

**Step 4 - Specially Designed
Pages are removed to reduce
thickness as you add photos**

Create Your Family
Travel Book Today!

Visit your local retailer,

use the order form in the back of this book,

or our website: www.kidslovepublications.com

Attention Parents:

All titles are "Kid Tested". *The authors and kids personally visited all of the most unique places* and wrote the books with warmth and excitement from a parent's perspective. Find tried and true places that children will enjoy. No more boring trips! Listings provide: Names, addresses, telephone numbers, websites, directions, and descriptions. All books include a bonus chapter listing state-wide kid-friendly Seasonal & Special Events!

❑ **KIDS LOVE INDIANA** - Discover places where you can "co-star" in a cartoon or climb a giant sand dune. Over 500 listings in one book about Indiana travel. 8 geographical zones, 213 pages.

❑ **KIDS LOVE KENTUCKY** - Discover places from Boone to Burgoo, from Caves to Corvettes, and from Lincoln to the Lands of Horses. Nearly 500 listings in one book about Kentucky travel. 5 geographic zones. 186 pages.

❑ **KIDS LOVE MICHIGAN** - Discover places where you can "race" over giant sand dunes, climb aboard a lighthouse "ship", eat at the world's largest breakfast table, or watch yummy foods being made. Almost 600 listings in one book about Michigan travel. 8 geographical zones, 229 pages.

❑ **KIDS LOVE OHIO** - Discover places like hidden castles and whistle factories. Over 800 listings in one book about Ohio travel. 9 geographical zones, 260 pages.

❑ **KIDS LOVE PENNSYLVANIA** - Explore places where you can "discover" oil and coal, meet Ben Franklin, or watch your favorite toys and delicious, fresh snacks being made. Over 900 listings in one book about Pennsylvania travel. 9 geographical zones, 268 pages.

❑ **KIDS LOVE TENNESSEE** – Explore places where you can "discover" pearls, ride the rails, "meet" Three Kings (of Rights, Rock & Soul). Be inspired to sing listening to the rich traditions of Country music fame. Over 500 listings in one book about Tennessee travel. 6 geographical zones, 235 pages.

❑ **KIDS LOVE THE VIRGINIAS** – Discover where ponies swim and dolphins dance, dig into archaeology and living history, or be dazzled by record-breaking and natural bridges. Over 900 listings in one book about Virginia & West Virginia travel. 8 geographical zones, 262 pages.

ORDER FORM

KIDS LOVE PUBLICATIONS

1985 Dina Court
Powell, Ohio 43065
(614) 792-6451
Visit our website: **www.kidslovepublications.com**

#	Title		Price	Total
	Kids Love Indiana		$13.95	
	Kids Love Kentucky		$13.95	
	Kids Love Michigan		$13.95	
	Kids Love Ohio		$13.95	
	Kids Love Pennsylvania		$13.95	
	Kids Love Tennessee		$13.95	
	Kids Love the Virginias		$13.95	
	Kids Love Travel Memories!		$14.95	
	Combo Discount Pricing			
	Combo #2 - Any 2 Books		$23.95	
	Combo #3 - Any 3 Books		$33.95	
	Combo #4 - Any 4 Books		$42.95	
			Subtotal	
	*(Please make check or money order payable to: **KIDS LOVE PUBLICATIONS**)*	*(Ohio Residents Only – Your local rate)*	Local/State Sales Tax	
	☐ Master Card ☐ Visa	*$2.00 first book $1.00 each additional*	Shipping	
			TOTAL	

Account Number ☐☐☐☐-☐☐☐☐-☐☐☐☐-☐☐☐☐

Exp Date: ☐☐/☐☐ (Month/Year)
Cardholder's Name _____
Signature *(required)* _____

Name: _____
Address: _____
City: _____ State: _____
Zip: _____ Telephone: _____

All orders are shipped within 2 business days of receipt by US Mail. If you wish to have your books autographed, please include a legible note with the message you'd like written in your book. Your satisfaction is 100% guaranteed or simply return your order for a prompt refund. Thanks for your order. Happy Exploring!

"Where to go?, What to do?, and How much will it cost?", are all questions that they have heard throughout the years from friends and family. These questions became the inspiration that motivated them to research, write and publish the "Kids Love" travel series.

This adventure of writing and publishing family travel books has taken them on a journey of experiences that they never could have imagined. They have appeared as guests on hundreds of radio and television shows, had featured articles in statewide newspapers and magazines, spoken to thousands of people at schools and conventions, and write monthly columns in many publications talking about "family friendly" places to travel.

George Zavatsky and Michele (Darrall) Zavatsky were raised in the Midwest and have lived in many different cities. They currently reside in a suburb of Columbus, Ohio. They feel very blessed to be able to create their own career that allows them to research, write and publish a series of best-selling kids' travel books. Besides the wonderful adventure of marriage, they place great importance on being loving parents to Jenny & Daniel.